REDEFINING FINANCIAL FREEDOM

A GOSPEL-BASED APPROACH TO MONEY

Chad S. Hamilton

PFI Publishing
DENVER, CO

PFI Publishing
3544 Yosemite St.
Denver, CO 80238
www.RedefiningFinancialFreedom.com

Ordering Information:
Quantity sales. Special discounts are available on quantity purchases by corporations, associations, and others. For details, contact the "Special Sales Department" at the address above.

Redefining Financial Freedom/Chad Hamilton. —1st ed.
ISBN 978-0-6926628-9-2

Contents

Dedicated to Jennifer, Quincey, Harper & Dylan

"You will know the truth & the truth will set you free."

—John 8:32

INTRODUCTION

S upposedly, Mark Twain had recurring dreams of lying on his bed as he was being suffocated by a huge Bible resting on his chest. The message implied by that imagery is pretty widespread even if the dream itself is not. The Bible is often perceived as repressive; like a straightjacket that constrains us and keeps us from doing what we really want to do.

The pervasive view in our culture is that Christianity – or any traditional religion for that matter – prevents us from being truly free. One hundred fifty years ago atheists started widely embracing the term "free thinkers," arguing that only by escaping from the realm of religion can anyone be free. This basic premise resonates even more in our current environment, which cherishes individual autonomy above all else.

So, what are we to make of the essential New Testament message that "Christ has set us free" (Galatians 5:1)? Scripture is not saying that we need to choose between freedom and faith in God. It is saying that freedom is actually predicated on faith in God.

There is a clear disconnect between what our culture says about freedom and what the Bible says about it. In our culture where most people view freedom as the power to do whatever you please and determine your own identity, it is not surprising to find resistance to the claim that obedience and trust in God is the path to freedom.

Instead, material wealth is viewed as the single greatest means for escaping from the control or power of others. According to dominant cultural views, the surest path to freedom is money. Those with the greatest financial means can exhibit the most freedom.

Testing out this hypothesis should not be incredibly difficult. If we look at people who have suddenly become wealthy, we should be able to observe a significant increase in freedom. So what about those who either inherited significant wealth or won the lottery? What do their lives look like before and after?

Mark Abramson is a sociologist at the University of Connecticut who studied the attitudes of lottery winners and the effect it had on people's attitudes toward success and work. He found that the more money a lottery winner received, the more likely it was that the person's life would fall apart. Here's how he explained it: [1]

> *"It was after about two years--18 months to two years--that you began to see some effect... The more people won, the more they seemed disenchanted with conventional success, aspirations."*

This is consistent with lots of other research on the well-being of lottery winners. One of the most common observations of those who have won the lottery is that they tend to spend all their money and go into debt. The other frequent observation is that their social relationships become much more strained.

So what is the root of the problem? Nelson Aldrich, the author of *Old Money*, attributes it to having "too many choices" and goes on to explain the implications of that: [2]

> *"(It) means that they never have to commit to anything. Whether it's a profession or wife or place of residence or a group of friends. They can always check out when the going gets a little difficult and not suffer any consequences for it. And in fact give themselves the illusion that they're lighting out for*

the territories. ... That sort of vast buffet of options is what keeps them uneasy, unproductive, and by and large focused on the one promise of wealth that this country understands, which is freedom."

The author John Sedgwick speaks of "learned helplessness," a term borrowed from the studies of psychologist Martin Seligman, as he described the following scenario: [3]

"Children brought up in luxury, with every need taken care of, lose, or never find, the ability to take care of themselves in any meaningful way."

One of the all-time great songwriters seemed to have noticed a similar problem. In "Like a Rolling Stone," Bob Dylan famously sang about "Miss Lonely" – a woman who was described like the aforementioned inheritors only to fall from grace and experience much more difficult financial circumstances. [4]

He summed up the effect of her reversal of fortune with the line: *"When you ain't got nothing, you got nothing to lose."* According to Dylan, the change in circumstances – and the corresponding loss of wealth – ultimately served to free her.

His character became free only after she lost everything; at which point she was no longer perpetually worried about her image, status, and money. Dylan implies that riches, far from liberating us, actually enslave us.

There is a reason why the cliché "the trappings of wealth" implies a type of bondage. A few years after Dylan wrote those words, another rock and roll icon, Janis Joplin echoed his sentiment when she belted out that *"freedom's just another word for nothing left to lose."* [5]

Dylan and Joplin certainly offered an important insight about how the more you have to lose, the more inclined you are to cling to it and, consequently, the less free you will be. Still it's not the whole truth.

Illusions of Freedom

The author David Foster Wallace described in a commencement address how we are all like fish who are unaware of the existence of the water they are swimming in. He said that the entire value of a liberal arts education is all about: [6]

> *"How to keep you from going through your comfortable, prosperous, respectable adult life dead, unconscious, a slave to your head and to your natural default setting of being uniquely, completely, imperially alone, day in and day out."*

On average, people watch nearly five hours of television per day, have their smart phones within five feet of their bodies at all times, and check their phones every five minutes. Amidst a barrage of entertainment and distractions, many of us are not even aware of how we are being shaped and influenced. But at a more macro level, the effects are easier to see, such as a 400% increase in the number of people taking antidepressant medication since 1988. [7]

Scripture assumes we will all obey something or someone. The only question is whether we choose intentional obedience to God or unintentional obedience to sin (Romans 6:16). Sin, of course, is not a fashionable concept. But, at a core level, it simply means we are worshipping something other than God.

Wallace was not a follower of Jesus, but he understood and articulated the idea that even atheists worship. He said it is not a question of "if" we will worship something but only a question of "what" we will worship. He then went on to warn against the *"kind of worship you just gradually slip into, day after day..."* [8]

According to the Bible, we are all – at a fundamental level – desiring beings, and we shape our lives around whatever we love most. That's why sin is ultimately a matter of "disordered loves," as St. Augustine put it. When we love certain things and individuals more than we love God, we are sinning. We are also made into servants of whatever it is we love most. We just don't know it.

In terms of unpopular concepts, the notion of conformity is right up there with sin. But the fact is we all conform to certain limitations. It is not possible to live without doing so. The right types of limitations are absolutely essential in order to be free.

Consider the great American road trip. It symbolizes the essence of freedom, but it's just not at all accurate to think it is an escape from all constraints. Your car is not going to go far, and you are never going to experience much, if you don't adhere to the confines of the road itself and basic traffic laws. As Frank Turner declares in his aptly named song, "The Road," *"Only being shackled to the road could ever I be free."*[9]

Even the most creative work is dependent on limitations. Budgets, deadlines, or highly specific restrictions around the process all help in managing energy and executing ideas. The projects most likely to fail are those which are completely open-ended with no deadlines. As Scott Belsky contends in his book, *Making Ideas Happen:*[10]

> *"Brilliant creative minds become more focused and actionable when the realm of possibilities is defined and, to some extent, restricted."*

In terms of artistic expression, improv acting may seem to epitomize freedom and creativity. But while improv actors appear to be completely unbound by restrictions, in reality each actor is submitting to the narrative introduced by the actor before him so as to continue the evolving story line.

Watching great jazz musicians improvise together gives the appearance of total freedom from any limits. But even as they create beautiful music on the fly, the individual musicians are actually all adhering to the same basic rhythmic and melodic structures. Those structures are essential in order to play together. As Pastor (and musician) Robert Gelinas says, jazz musicians are *"Bound by the song but not constrained by it."* [11]

The point is, even in these situations that seem (on the surface) to exemplify freedom and a lack of limitations, there are healthy limits and a certain framework that must be adhered to in order to be truly free. Freedom and creativity require proper limitations combined with independence and autonomy.

It is also true, however, that most religions hamper true freedom because they are based on systems of rules and behavioral practices. They are about an endless pressure to perform; to earn God's favor.

Real Freedom

"I am Yahweh your God who brought you out of Egypt out of the house of slavery." – Exodus 20:2

Unlike all other religions, the Christian faith is built on grace. It is not about being bound by an ever-growing set of rules but about God's boundless grace and love for us. We are given Commandments, not so that we can earn his love, but rather as a sort of owner's manual for how humanity works.

Oil changes, tire replacement, and tune-ups are things we do to avoid being broken down on the side of the road. Likewise, God's commands allow us to avoid breaking down - spiritually, emotionally, and physically. But not only that, they facilitate the path of freedom.

6

When asked what was the greatest commandment, Jesus said it was to *"love the Lord your God with all your heart, all your soul, and all your mind."* And then, secondarily, *"you should love your neighbor as yourself."* Christ declared that all the law and the prophets hang on these two commandments. Notice they are not negative injunctions; these commands are positive visions for humanity centered around love as the defining action.

As such, "Thou shalt not steal" hangs on the commandment to love God and love neighbor. The commandment against stealing is not a narrow prohibition pertaining to a certain type of behavior. It is about not robbing God, the owner of everything, and not acting as though everything is ours to do what we want with it.

It is an injunction against leveraging the desperation of the poor and underprivileged. That is why the prohibition against robbery in Ezekial 18:7 is connected with the obligation to give food to the hungry and provide clothing for the naked. It is ultimately about justice. It is about what it means to actually love people with our financial resources.

The 10th Commandment addresses the topic of covetousness. It is about an orienting desire - what moves us toward action. It should not be interpreted as a command not to covet (or desire) in general. Instead it is admonishing certain types of desires. We are not supposed to orient our lives around a longing for things that are not ours.

However, we cannot simply cease from having certain desires. Christ showed us something that our culture does not understand about human nature. Our hearts are idol factories, as John Calvin put it. Our hearts will always lead us to worship something. We will end up centering our lives upon something or someone. It is inevitable. And it is this realization of human nature which forms the basis for scripture's teaching on the topic of freedom.

Instead of eliminating misplaced desires, we need to replace them. It is not about shrinking or reigning in our desires but about magnifying our desires in a different direction (toward God's new world breaking into the midst of the old). We are to do this not, primarily, out of a sense of duty but out of a sense love. In so doing, we should discern how our loves are being shaped and moved in ways that are in conflict with God's purposes.

Under the influence of covetousness and envy, our lives can become about maintaining our image, rather than about loving our neighbors as we love ourselves. The commandment is ultimately a call for our longings to be aligned with God's desires. We must become enamored with God's vision for the world.

Three Money Questions

In a way, this is an iconoclastic book. It is an attack on one of the most cherished beliefs in our culture – that money and riches is the key to happiness. Instead, we are taking a subversive approach and turning these false stories on their heads: taking an upside-down narrative and turning it right side up.

For the last 20 years, I've worked in the wealth management industry which is basically predicated on the premise of helping clients achieve financial freedom. But the freedom being offered by countless publications and financial gurus is illusory when it is based solely on mathematical calculations.

Instead, we need to address a central question: Why are we making the financial decisions we are making? What is the motivation behind these decisions?

To go about identifying these motivations, the book is organized around three questions designed to reveal problems and present gospel-based solutions with regard to how you approach your personal finances. As it pertains to money, we ask:

I. **How did you get it?**

    (How we think about work)

II. **What are you doing with it?**

    (Considerations for investing)

III. **What is it doing to you?**

    (Importance of giving & generosity)

A Pendulum

To answer these questions, we use the central metaphor of a pendulum. It swings between two extremes; with apathy on one end and idolatry on the other.

On the one hand, we can minimize the role and importance of money and say it really is no big deal (the end of the pendulum characterized as "apathy"). But this betrays the Biblical perspective which contends that it is, in fact, a very big deal.

Scripture makes it abundantly clear that money – or Mammon as Christ referred to it – possesses a spiritual power. It represents a very real and very dangerous force that can enslave our hearts. It can put us under its bondage. Jesus explained that a rich man has about as much chance of going to heaven as a camel through the eye of the needle and told the rich young ruler that he must give away everything to follow Him.

If you are a follower of Christ living in the most prosperous nation in the history of the world right now and those verses do not send a shiver up your spine, you are either not reading carefully enough or you are choosing to rationalize away what Christ is saying. Those are the only options. Otherwise, it is chilling.

This is a matter of utmost importance. And yet, how many of us would actually have pause in considering what a big promotion or inheritance might do to our soul? The point is we do not take it seriously enough in terms of the power of money to warp our priorities and enslave us. It is much more than a medium of exchange, it is a spiritual power.

Yet, we can swing to the other side of the pendulum ("idolatry") and attribute way too much importance to money. In this case, it has too tight of a grip on us. We hoard it and covet it. We may even exploit or oppress others to get it. Marriages end because of it. Families are ripped apart in battles surrounding it. Wars are fought for it. The list, of course, could go on, but the point is the pursuit of money is made into something of far greater importance than it deserves.

No human life should have a price tag, but that is essentially what happens. In a world where money is taken too seriously, everything and everyone is commoditized. Why? Because money is seen as the channel toward which we will find our ultimate hopes.

It is not as if we make one mistake or the other. Instead, the pendulum tends to swing back and forth in what amounts to futility and a lack of any real progress or change for most of us, most of the time. We tend to make both mistakes by underestimating what money can do to us (apathy) while overestimating what money can do for us (idolatry).

Jesus devoted more than 15% of his recorded words to the topic of money. Why is that? He wants us to be free. Free from the widespread cultural idolatry of money. Free from the false assumptions we subconsciously accept from our culture pertaining to money.

What we do with our money reveals a whole lot about us. The things we care about, what we think will make us happy, and where we put our trust. The Bible contains more than 2,300 verses about money.

How we handle our money and possessions is a window into our soul. Billy Graham once declared, *"Give me 5 minutes with a person's checkbook and I will tell you where their heart is."*

Money talks. So what is it saying about you? Let's find out.

REDEFINING FINANCIAL FREEDOM

Section I

First Money Question:

How Did You Get It?

(How we think about WORK)

CHAPTER 1

Missing the Point

When I was in high school, I was given a number of reading assignments of classic literature, including some of the greats by Charles Dickens, Mark Twain, and Shakespeare. I can't recall actually reading a single one of them in their entirety. I was only concerned with understanding whatever was necessary to pass the tests or write the necessary reports on those books. Therefore, I would buy the "Cliff Notes" (I'm not even sure if such a thing exists anymore, but imagine something like hard copy versions of Wikipedia entries pre-internet age).

I was not interested in the books themselves, I was interested only in learning whatever I needed in order to get good grades in my class. So I would short circuit the process as much as possible and then move on.

Fast forward 20+ years and I now voluntarily read those same books that I never read back then. Except that now I have no tests afterward. I write no reviews. These books offer me no clearly discernable impact on my career advancement or financial gains. So, why do I want to read *Huckleberry Finn* now (much less *War and Peace!*) when I have nothing "practical" to gain from it?

Because great literature is a window into the soul of humanity. There are essential truths contained in those great books written decades or centuries ago that shed light on struggles that still happen every day in very different times and places. These writers so keenly understood human nature that they help me understand myself better through their great characters. As I empathize with them – their struggles and their passions – I learn more about what it means to truly love and care about people. I learn how I fall short in so many ways and how deeply broken I am. And I learn about God in powerful ways.

But what changed for me? These books certainly haven't. It is only my perspective that changed. I used to read them (or peruse them) only as a means to an end. I concerned myself with only the practical, short term considerations. I had no concern about these novels for their own sake. The difference is that I now read these books as an end in and of themselves.

CHAPTER 2

The Efficiency Obsession

We live in a world that is increasingly obsessed with efficiency and practicality. And that has implications for how we live and interact with others and how we think. It has implications for how we view our work as well.

Oscar Wilde famously quipped that only the superficial do not judge by appearances.[1] He was referring to this problem – this obsession with practicality. In search of efficiency and results, we lack imagination and miss the beauty that is right in front of us. This is an area where we can learn a lot from children. My three year-old son looks at water dripping out of a rusty old drainage pipe and calls it a waterfall.

G.K. Chesterton once said, *"The world will never starve for want of wonders but only want of wonder."*[2] When we are too focused on getting things done and optimizing our time, the result is a failure to truly see things that are right in front of us.

In school I missed out on the beauty of the words and stories in my hands because I looked at them as only a means to an end. Similarly, we are constantly tempted to make the same mistake when it comes to the topic of work. We often view it as a means to an end.

Now, the interesting thing is that work can be viewed as a means to an end in two very different ways. If I view my job as merely what I do in order to pay for the things I *really* want to do, my work is a means to an end. Interestingly, the same is true for the opposite end of the spectrum. If my work defines who I am, it is also a means to an end. The end in that case is career advancement or promotion. Or it is about quenching a need for respect and admiration at work.

CHAPTER 3

Work as a Chore

ccording to Gallup's 2016 research on work satisfaction, only 13% of workers across the world and 30% of U.S. workers felt engaged by their jobs.[3] These are people who have a sense of passion for work and actively look for ways to help move the organization forward. Large majorities are not engaged, meaning they are checked out or putting little energy into their work. The remainder is actively disengaged. These people say they either hate their work or are extremely frustrated with it.

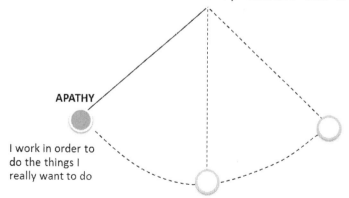

APATHY

I work in order to
do the things I
really want to do

In the mid-70's, author and historian Studs Terkel published a book called *Working*. It documents the results of hundreds of interviews with people in all types of professions. Terkel asked questions to understand their views about work. One of the interviewees is Hobart Foote, a 37 year-old utility man who worked the day shift at an auto plant for the previous 17 years. He said this: [4]

> *"The company puts bread and butter on the table. I feed the family and with two teen-aged kids, there's a lot of wants. And we're paying for two cars. And I have brought home a forty-hour paycheck for Lord knows how long. And that's why I work."*

Foote's synopsis of work – both its purpose and his attitudes toward it – is indicative of the majority of people interviewed in *Working*. Individuals who fall into this category have a bifurcated view of work and life. What they do for a living is a "job" rather than a "career" or a "calling." It is compartmentalized in the sense that they work to receive the pay and/or benefits to support their hobbies, family, or life outside work. They prefer jobs which do not interfere with their personal lives. They are not as likely to have a strong connection to the workplace or their job duties. The job serves only as a basic necessity in life.

In this case, work can often be frustrating because it is lacking in meaning and purpose. It is a requirement that is done or put up with in order to enjoy the rest of life. Work is a four letter word that must be endured in order to reap its benefits. This is revealed in studies such as Gallup's which reveal that large majorities of people across the world are not engaged at work.

CHAPTER 4

A Disconnect

A
t the beginning of his Sermon on the Mount, Jesus declares, *"Blessed are the poor in spirit, for theirs is the kingdom of God."* It implies a radical dependency on God. The posture of the "poor in spirit" is someone who comes to God with the dependent humility of a child. It means acknowledging our spiritual poverty before God. We deserve nothing from him and we have nothing to offer Him that he does not already have. We are poor in spirit when we come to God with empty hands.

In a culture obsessed with self-promotion and self-aggrandizement, this can be good news indeed. If all that we have is provided by God's grace, we can escape the treadmill of performance. It's a great corrective against a mindset driven by meritocracy, which works in opposition to love and grace. In an often overworked and overstressed environment where we tend to put insurmountable burdens on our own shoulders, this is a source of freedom. We are not co-contributors to our own redemption.

And yet, when coupled with a lack of understanding of the importance of calling and vocation, it can result in apathy. We can fall prey to a mindset that says our actions do not really matter and our work does not really matter. This is a lie that must be debunked head-on if we are to avoid living a bifurcated life where our professed faith on Sundays bears little resemblance to our lives from Monday through Friday. Understanding the absolute centrality and significance of work is crucial to integrating our faith with the rest of life.

What Dorothy Sayers said three generations ago still rings true today: [5]

> "In nothing has the church so lost her hold on reality as in her failure to understand and respect the secular vocation. She has allowed work and religion to become separate departments, and is astonished to find that, as a result, the secular work of the world is turned to purely selfish and destructive ends, and that the greater part of the world's intelligent workers have become irreligious, or at least, uninterested in religion. But is it that astonishing? How can anyone remain interested in a religion which seems to have no concern for nine-tenths of life? The church's approach to an intelligent carpenter is usually confined to exhorting him to not be drunk and disorderly in his leisure hours, and to come to church on Sundays. What the church should be telling him is this: that the very first demand that his religion makes on him it to make good tables."

We cannot experience financial freedom if the central activity which provides financial resources is something we merely "put up with" or even suffer through. True freedom is not contingent on a change in circumstances. Freedom cannot be predicated on a financial windfall or someday being able to quit working. To be free is not to be liberated from work but rather to be liberated in work. And that requires us to avoid having an indifferent attitude toward it.

CHAPTER 5

Work as an Idol

P salm 8:5-8 explains that all of humanity is given power and dominion to rule. The creation account in Genesis also makes it perfectly clear that we are designed to work, and that our work has a divine purpose.

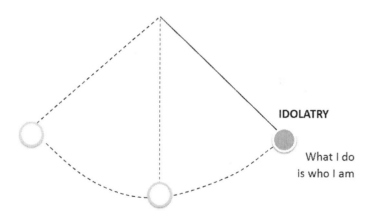

IDOLATRY

What I do
is who I am

Yet this understanding can easily become skewed and lead to an overemphasis on our own efforts, abilities, and power. When we consider common career aspirations, they are often focused on elements related to success or prestige. We may be interested in moving up a corporate ladder, receiving a raise or a promotion, or achieving the social standing that comes with a new position.

In this case, work is often stifling or oppressive because identity and self-worth is tied to it. The politics of work are often likely to restrain a person from taking risks or expressing any truly unique opinions. As Matthew Crawford put it in *Shop Class as Soulcraft*: [6]

> *"Workers find ingenious ways to avoid taking responsibility mainly by making their language as vague and empty as possible so as to preserve for themselves a maximum flexibility to reinterpret their utterances retroactively should the circumstances demand it."*

It sounds like the description of a typical politician. For those of us who have spent any significant amount of time in Corporate America, it will also sound like a familiar description of certain co-workers. What it most certainly does not sound like is a truly free individual. Overly cautious self-censorship in order not to offend or be proven wrong is the recipe for groupthink that is quite common in many organizations.

In this type of environment, bland value propositions and marketing materials are created in order to avoid taking the risk of saying something truly unique. It tends to be very conventional and uncreative. To the most politically saavy workers, this makes perfect sense. The mantra is some variant of "Keep your head down, don't take any big risks, and make the right impressions on the right people." To those looking for meaning, purpose, and true excellence in their work, it is dispiriting.

There is also the simple fact that when those whose greatest aspiration is to climb the ladder actually reach the top, they are left wanting more. In Terkel's book, he interviewed a man named Larry Ross, who was described as an "ex-president of a conglomerate." Ross said, [7]

> *"The corporation is a jungle. It's exciting. You're thrown in on your own and you're constantly battling to survive. When you learn to survive, the game is to become the conqueror, the leader."*

He then went on to explain what it felt like once he had reached the pinnacle of success at his company.

> *"I left that world because suddenly the power and the status were empty. I'd been there, and when I got there it was nothing."*

CHAPTER 6

Barriers to Freedom

A s we alluded to earlier, both ends of the pendulum suffer from the same core problem. Whether your view of work is merely utilitarian (ex: it pays the bills) or your primary source of self-worth (ex: it defines me), work is viewed as merely a means to an end.

Work is attributed with too little importance when it is viewed only as a means of getting paid or punching a clock. Conversely, work is assigned too great of an importance when it is the source of one's identity.

Either way, a person is not truly free. He is bound by work – either as a necessary evil that must be endured or as an essential means of defining oneself and one's worth.

In the former case, the majority of a person's waking hours are spent doing something just so other, enjoyable experiences can be attained. In the latter case, a person may feel confined so much by pressure to move up the ladder and advance, that he or she is not free to express true opinions for fear of political fallout. In that case, tactical considerations may trap this person into being someone (s)he is not.

So what does true freedom in work look like?

CHAPTER 7

A Calling

To understand the Biblical perspective of work, we need to understand the meaning of "calling." Often the term is used to simply mean job or career, but it is much more than that. Those with a calling orientation consider their work to be integral to their lives. They view their career as a form of self-expression, personal fulfillment, and service toward a greater purpose. These people are primarily driven by internal aspirations.

Dr. Amy Wrzesniewski is an Associate Professor of Organizational Behavior at Yale University's School of Management. In research done with several colleagues, she discovered that individuals with a calling orientation are more likely to find their work meaningful and will modify their duties and develop relationships to make it more so.[8] They are found to be more satisfied in general with their work and their lives.

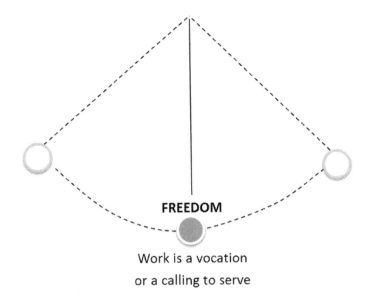

FREEDOM

Work is a vocation
or a calling to serve

But it is important to understand that calling is less about us than it is about God. In order to be called, there must be a "caller." Few things are as remarkable as the Creator of the Universe stooping down to summon us. In Isaiah 43:1, the Lord says *"Fear not, for I have redeemed you; I have called you by name, you are mine."* This sense of calling serves as a strong rebuttal against the inclination to have a compartmentalized and dismissive view of work and its importance in our lives.

Of course, this still leaves us susceptible to the temptation of making a career a source of identity or an idol. The fundamental way in which that can be avoided is by understanding the nature of calling. We are called by the sheer grace of God to use our gifts and abilities in a certain way. In order to have gifts, there must be a "giver" which again reinforces the fact of God's grace. If we understand that, at the root of our calling, is God's grace and our sheer dependence on him, we can avoid the temptation toward idolatry.

The implication of work as a vocation or calling is that work is an end in and of itself. As a result, there is greater emphasis on the beauty of the work I am creating and products I am producing. As human beings made in the image of the Creator, we, too, are wired to create. That's a key part of our role as humans and certainly key to understanding work.

For a stay at home mom, her work is, in part, a charge to create order from chaos in terms of interpersonal relationships (mediating disagreements), personal appearance (combing hair), and hospitality (washing dishes, cleaning). The entrepreneur creates wealth and jobs. The engineer designs and helps facilitate the creation of highways and bridges that enable us to travel. The carpenter restores a fragile antique piece of furniture. The science teacher creates a paradigm shifting recognition in the mind of a fifth grader as she is learning about the nature of atoms.

This act of creating lies at the core of our purpose for working. Serving is the other key aspect. Through our calling, we are able to fulfill the great commandments to love God and love others by creating and serving. This has the benefit of liberating us by providing us with a true pursuit, a passion that drives us toward a true purpose.

Ultimately, there is more purpose and meaning in the work being done; not because it serves some narrow self-interest, but because the work itself is important. As Aristotle said, "Where your talents and the needs of the world cross, there lies your calling."

People have an innate need to feel valued and to do something that matters. We actually expect this of others as well. As the psychologist Barry Schwartz has wittily noted, when we say that someone is *"just in it for the money,"* we are not merely being descriptive.[9]

The key to understanding the true importance of vocation from a theological perspective starts with eschatology and a simple question. What is the scope of redemption? Is God interested in merely saving souls or redeeming all things? The answer to that question leads to a definition of how we define ministry.

If God is concerned only with the salvation of our souls, the implication is that ministry is limited to church stuff. If, on the other hand, God is ultimately going to redeem and restore all things (the earth, our bodies, society, relationships) then the definition is expanded to include all things that bring glory to God. That now means that all kinds of work have the potential to be ministry.

CHAPTER 8

Cleaning Up

Some people are reading this and thinking, "Yeah, that sounds great for the privileged few who are at liberty to selectively pursue specific passions and capitalize on them to earn a living. But what about those of us who do not have the good fortune to be in a situation where our gifts are perfectly utilized?" What about blue-collar jobs or what is considered more mundane work?

In 2001, Amy Wrzesniewski began to study how people in undesirable jobs were able to effectively cope with devalued and poorly compensated work. She had detailed conversations with the custodial staff at a hospital about their jobs, and she discovered a subset of people who didn't see themselves as part of the janitorial staff. [10]

Instead, they viewed themselves as part of the professional staff and as a crucial part of the healing team. Wrzesniewski used the term "job crafting" to describe this observation. It means that, instead of changing your work, you carefully and intentionally craft how you think about your work.

One custodial worker observed which patients seemed to have few visitors and would then make sure to double back to spend some time with them. Another worker stopped mopping the floors in an area where a patient was recovering from major surgery and was getting some much-needed exercise by slowly walking up and down the halls. Similarly, there was a custodial worker who refrained from vacuuming the visitor's lounge because some family members were napping. He did this in spite of his supervisor's warnings because he knew the exhausted family members had been there all day.

David Sturt, author of the book *Great Work*, says, [11]

> *"To reframe one's job is to make a mental connection with a grander purpose: Its social benefit. Its worth to society. Its potential to benefit others. Thinking of the good our work can do, beyond our daily to-do list, helps us change how we relate to our work."*

Jeff Haanen, the founder of Denver Institute for Faith & Work, puts it this way: [12]

> *"Tensions in our work will remain. But hope for... meaningful work won't be found in self-actualization but instead in the freedom of self-forgetfulness."*

CHAPTER 9

Police Work

Officer Tommy Norman has been with the North Little Rock Police Department of Arkansas since 1998. He's become legendary for a commitment to his community that goes beyond what any of us expect from police officers. He is a white police officer in a predominantly African-American community.

On any given day, he's being chased down the street by throngs of kids screaming his name. Certainly, it helps that he fills the trunk of his squad car with cold drinks and toys that he routinely gives away. But that is not what ultimately endears these children to him. It is his absolute dedication to them.

Officer Norman knows all of the children by name and notices when someone is missing or not doing well. He serves the community out of a deep sense of love and commitment. On any given day, you can see him on Instagram visiting an elderly neighbor or going to a kid's birthday party and sporting event. He lets the children sit in his police car, wear his badge, and even turn on the siren.

The community's deeply rooted admiration for Norman is apparent in his many videos. Without being prompted, the children address him as "Sir." The body language, giggles, and teasing of their favorite officer are evidence that they feel a sense of peace and comfort around him.

In inner cities across the country, police departments struggling to build trust and legitimacy in their communities could learn a lot from Officer Norman. With thousands of postings on social media, he's gone viral for all the right reasons. As it turns out, authentic relationships like these do not just make us feel good; they have a positive effect on the crime rate itself. Norman puts it this way, [13]

> *"When you become friends with a child, when they think about breaking the law, they know you will be upset and that they will disappoint you, and they think twice before doing that."*

Norman acts as a friend and even a father figure to many children. Because these children know that he cares for them, they want to make him proud. In the context of a positive relationship, they are also taught that they have value, potential, and a future. Because of this, Norman says, *"My tickets are down and my arrests are down — but the hope and the promise, they're up."*

When one follower asked Norman "When do you have time to do police work?" he simply responded by saying "This is police work."

CHAPTER 10

Creative Imagination

In 2010, Rachel Starkey came across bags filled with 'off-cuts' waste outside a textiles factory and was inspired to reuse this waste for a new purpose. Starkey and her husband had started a garment manufacturing business in Egypt in 2002, and so she had ideas for how discarded fabric could be utilized. She envisioned this fabric being recycled from waste into opportunity for people living on less than two dollars per day.

Rachel felt strongly about the growing school drop-out rate amongst young African girls due to the lack of adequate sanitary solutions. In Kenya, 65% of girls 18 years and younger have dropped out of school. Without feminine hygiene protection girls miss six weeks of school per year, which contributes significantly to the dropout rate. In one study in Uganda conducted by Oxford University, girls who were provided menstrual protection increased their attendance rates by 75%. [14]

To help solve this problem, Rachel Starkey and her husband founded Transformation Textiles. They originally started by producing simple, reusable pads from discarded fabric. They have now expanded into producing "dignity kits" which include all the basic supplies needed by girls and women to remain in work or school.

Its mission is:

- To reach and impact the emerging generation of Africa's young women.
- To provide them with high quality, affordable feminine hygiene products so they can remain in school and complete their education.
- To empower them to break the cycle of poverty and to place value upon womanhood.

Antoine de Saint-Exupery once wrote, *"A rock pile ceases to be a rock pile the moment a single man contemplates it, bearing within him the image of a cathedral."* Similarly, Rachel Starkey said, *"Some people only see leftover scraps of fabric... I see a whole generation of girls that get to stay in school."* [15]

Jessica Jackley co-founded the micro-lending platform, Kiva, and expressed this redemptive interpretation of the entrepreneurial vision: [16]

> *"In their own way, great entrepreneurs have to develop their faith muscles. We may use different language and talk about imagination or being visionary. But there's something about that that's very familiar to me, that has a lot to do with the invisible Truth of the world. I believe entrepreneurship has an amazing, redemptive attitude and framework. It teaches us how to live life in a way that is solution-finding and hopeful and optimistic and constantly redeeming the world. It's about creating something from nothing, about creating value."*

CHAPTER 11

Great Products

If we think about visionary companies of the early 21st Century, few are as compelling as Apple. It is an example of a company that has historically put products before profits.

Steve Jobs was notorious for his relentless focus on the beauty and value of products rather than viewing them as just a vehicle to drive profit maximization.

When Jobs returned to Apple in the late 1990's, he shifted the company's focus back to making innovative products. These ground-breaking products ranged from the iMac to the iPod and then, ultimately, the iPhone and the iPad. As he explained, *"My passion has been to build an enduring company where people were motivated to make great products. Everything else was secondary."* [17]

For all his many personal faults, Jobs understood that work needed to be about the products being produced not the financial success that you hoped to achieve from those products. The work product was the end goal; not merely a means to the end of making money. As Jobs summarized:

"Sure, it was great to make a profit, because that was what allowed you to make great products. But the products, not the profits, were the motivation... It's a subtle difference, but it ends up meaning everything—the people you hire, who gets promoted, what you discuss in meetings."

There is great satisfaction that can come from creating things – whether these things are fine works of craftsmanship or intellectual solutions to intricate problems or PowerPoint presentations. This is not accidental; we were made to create – it is part of what we were designed to do.

CHAPTER 12

Rest

The most significant sign of true freedom in our work is being able to rest. St. Augustine famously said in his own *Confessions* to the Lord, *"Our hearts are restless until they rest in you."*[18]

The key to rest is not worrying about or feeling responsible for ultimate results, but instead being primarily concerned with being a faithful presence and then letting the chips fall where they may. This is not the same as a lack of accountability. Of course, deadlines must be met, tasks must be completed, and results must be achieved if at all possible. But those results that are out of our control are the ones that can wreak havoc and cause great anxiety.

Chapter 14 of the book of Acts recounts the story of how the apostles Paul and Barnabas bore witness for Jesus and performed miracles in the towns they visited. And yet, despite their faithfulness and even the healing of a man who was crippled from birth, the reaction of the crowd was mixed. Some came to believe in God, some believed in false Gods, and some reacted in hostility.

Doing what they were called to do did not result in unmitigated success. And yet, despite being stoned, dragged out of the city, and mistaken for dead, Paul was undeterred and ultimately thanked God for having "opened a door of faith to the Gentiles." Notice the wording – it is in reference to the opportunity given them by God to serve as faithful witnesses. Paul and Barnabas knew the bio of Jesus. They knew that their Lord also experienced a mixed bag of results. While many were saved by Him, others were indifferent and still more were hostile to his message, even to the point of killing him.

Still, neither Jesus nor the leaders of the early church were filled with anxiety over needing to achieve certain results. They were not obsessed with "winning." They were able to trust in God and his sovereignty and love which enabled them to rest even in the midst of discouraging results and perilous circumstances.

Only by trusting in God can we achieve meaningful rest. Isaiah 57:20 says the wicked are like the tossing sea when it cannot rest. God designed us to rest. It is important to understand that the Sabbath (and work itself) predates the fall. To rest is to cooperate with the way God has designed our bodies to operate. We are like power tools that need to be recharged.

Years ago, Judith Shulevitz wrote a great article in the *New York Times* called "Bring Back the Sabbath." In it, she dispelled many myths about the Sabbath and extolled the need for rest. In one particularly poignant passage, Shulevitz says: [19]

> *"Most people mistakenly believe that all you have to do to stop working is not work. The inventors of the Sabbath understood that it was a much more complicated undertaking. You cannot downshift casually and easily, the way you might slip into bed at the end of a long day. As the Cat in the Hat says, "It is fun to have fun but you have to know how." This is why the Puritan and Jewish Sabbaths were so exactingly intentional... The rules did not exist to torture the faithful. They were meant to communicate the insight that interrupting the ceaseless round of striving requires a surprisingly strenuous act of will, one that has to be bolstered by habit as well as by social sanction."*

In Deuteronomy 5:15, when the Sabbath is initially introduced as one of the Ten Commandments, it is positioned as an act of liberation ("therefore rest"). If your work defines your identity, you are enslaved. If dreams of escape from your work dominate your thoughts, you are enslaved. But if your work is meaningful while your ultimate hope and love is in Christ, you can rest.

That is what Jesus meant when he said in Matthew 11:28, "Come to me, all who labor and are heavy laden, and I will give you rest." That sounds like freedom to me.

Section II

Second Money Question:

What Are You Doing With It?

(Considerations for INVESTING)

CHAPTER 1

The Sacred-Secular Divide

In Mark 7:17-23, Jesus tells his disciples that it is not what goes into a man from the outside that defiles him but rather what comes out of him (i.e., avarice, wickedness, deceit, envy, pride, etc.). He was shifting the focus from external practices inwardly to the inclinations of the human heart. In doing so, Jesus upended Jewish tradition and religious practices by declaring that all foods are clean.

In effect, Jesus was rebuking the historical dividing line between the clean and the unclean. It would be easy to read these scenes and miss their significance for those of us living in the 21st century. Yet, this is not merely a rebuke of certain ancient ethnic distinctives of diet.

There is a consistent refrain in the New Testament that teaches us to avoid compartmentalizing the world into two separate realms: the sacred and the profane. It is understandable since the Old Covenant functioned this way and, prior to the saving grace of Jesus, there were stringent requirements and distinctions between the sacred and the unclean.

For us, in much less reverent or religious times, it is not so much a divide between the sacred and the profane but a divide between the spiritual and the ordinary or secular. Many of us unwittingly make a distinction between things that are holy and things that are worldly.

There are few people who would say they uphold and support maintaining a sharp distinction between the sacred and the secular. Most of us know intellectually and theologically it's not a Biblical concept. God is sovereign over everything; his sphere is not limited to whatever we label "spiritual" or "Christian."

Yet, there is subconscious distinction we make without even realizing it. It is why we tend to confine "ministry" to religious professions or certain "noble" nonprofit organizations. The importance of business and investing is then diminished as a result of the sacred-secular divide.

CHAPTER 2

The Purpose of Business

The biggest danger followers of Jesus have in terms of business and investing is not nefarious motives but unexamined assumptions. We take for granted certain cultural assumptions and are unaware of the dangers they pose. The unspoken and implied belief is that business is secular space – morally neutral at best or even a necessary evil that provides the wealth needed to fund ministries, missions, and so forth. The unintentional consequence of partitioning off business from theological concerns is an acceptance of thoroughly unbiblical perceptions of it.

Decades ago, Milton Friedman – along with many other influential economists – contended that business managers have a moral obligation to do everything within their power to maximize shareholder value. Since then, the conventional wisdom has coalesced around the idea that the primary purpose of business is to maximize profits.

Does the creation account in Genesis support this claim? Well, certainly there is a case to be made that business is designed to create value, enable prosperity, and even create wealth (Deuteronomy

8:17-18). When God commanded in Genesis 1:28 that we are to work the fields and cause the land to be "fruitful" and "fill the earth," we might well characterize this as wealth creation.

But the question really is one of purpose versus results. The purpose of business from a Biblical perspective is not to maximize profits. Profits are crucial to a business achieving its goals, but it is not its primary purpose.

Just as we need to eat to survive, businesses need profits to survive. However, it does not follow that businesses then exist in order to maximize profits. By that logic, nonprofit organizations exist to raise funds. After all, many nonprofit workers would say that is where they spend most of their time. And yet, no one is really confused about that when it comes to nonprofits. We all understand that, while fundraising is crucial to their survival, nonprofits exist in order to serve those in need.

In business, organizations lose much of their intrinsic worth and meaning if viewed as only a means to an end (maximizing profits or shareholder value). It can cause companies to lose focus on what truly matters (i.e., serving the needs of customers, creating great products, etc.) and concentrate on very short term results. This misguided short term focus can be intensified by Wall Street pressures.

Here's how Kenneth Cole described his company's experience after becoming publicly-traded: [1]

> "The Street is ruthless and unrelenting. Very often it distorts the process of why you do what you do. It demands a very short and immediate focus on quarterly results. There's no real relationship to sustainable, long-term objectives and goals. We found ourselves so focused on messaging that we lost track of how to elevate what we were doing. Rather than make the numbers better, we would talk about how to talk about them. There were all these various stakeholders, and their interests were not always aligned, so we would often have to figure out how to create a certain perception for the audience we were speaking to, rather than focus on how to be a better company." *

This is emblematic of the corrosive effect of short term decision-making which has the wrong end in mind when it comes to the purpose of business. If profit is understood to be an end in and of itself, then being truthful and straightforward with customers becomes expendable. Providing meaningful work to employees is optional. These goals are only prioritized to the extent that they help the bottom line.

That is clearly at odds with the Biblical vision for business. There is a reason why the Apostle Paul includes "swindling" among a select list of other sins such as sexual immorality, idolatry, and drunkenness. The word swindling referred to a ruthless business practice, but not an illegal one. And yet, Paul is intentional in making it clear that it is characteristic of *"wrongdoers who will not inherit the kingdom of God."* (1 Corinthians 5-6)

According to Jeff Van Duzer's excellent book, *Why Business Matters to God*, the primary purpose of business is twofold: [2] 1) to provide the community with goods and services that enable it to flourish and 2) to provide opportunities for meaningful work that enable people to utilize their God given abilities. The first is external; the second is internal.

Many of the best companies in the world are ones that put purpose before profit. They have a grand vision for making the world – or some small corner of it – somehow better off. The employees of these companies are doing work that matters to them.

In *Built to Last*, Jim Collins and Jerry Poras showed that organizations driven by purpose and values outperformed the general market 15:1.[3] Another book called *Firms of Endearment* identified thirty companies that are driven by a clear sense of purpose and that put their employees and customers ahead of the needs of shareholders. The stocks of these purpose-driven firms outperformed their more conventional competitors by a ratio of 8-to-1.[4]

Frank Reichheld, from Bain & Company, substantiated similar findings by arguing that companies driven by a strong sense of purpose outperform, while those transfixed on profit and shareholders underperform.[5] If this is true, it has major implications for how we should think about investing. Wise investing would then necessitate an evaluation of what purpose various businesses serve and what values they represent.

Incidentally, Cole took the company private again in 2012 after 18 years as a publicly-traded company.

CHAPTER 3

Values & Investing

If someone were to ask you to invest in a new business idea for opening a strip club, would you do it? Let's assume this is a potentially lucrative investment opportunity. Of course, it's doubtful any of us would proceed to make that type of investment. We would not rationalize it by saying we're just going to make as much money as possible so that we can have more money to give away.

Yet, the vast majority of self-professed Christians own shares of companies (often held within mutual funds) that directly profit from things like pornography and abortion-related products and services.

One reason for this is we've become far removed from our investments. Mutual funds own dozens or even hundreds of different companies, and it would be unreasonable to expect those who are not financial professionals to be able to monitor and track all of these underlying investments. As a result, most of us don't really know what we own and what types of values those companies espouse.

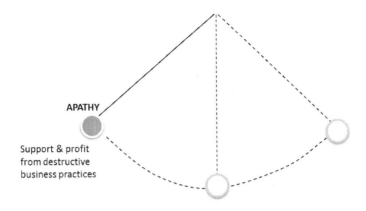

APATHY

Support & profit
from destructive
business practices

Fortunately, individuals no longer have to screen their own investments to ensure they align with their values; the number of investment options that offer a values-based screen has grown considerably. Ten years ago there were slightly more than 200 funds using environmental and social screening factors, while today there are approximately 1000.

By all indications, values-based investing is a growing trend. According to the Forum for Sustainable & Responsible Investment, $6.6 trillion is invested according to "sustainable, responsible, and impact investing." That is triple the amount from 15 years ago and more than double the amount in 2010. [6]

Nearly 6 in 10 affluent investors say the social and environmental impact of companies they invest in is important to their decision-making. For next generation investors, the topic is even more appealing: roughly three-quarters of those under the age of 40 say socially minded investing is important. [7]

Yet, despite the growing acceptance of values-oriented investing, many Christians are still hesitant to embrace it. The biggest single reason for this is the sacred-secular divide. We hear a lot in our churches about the importance of giving but very little about how we should earn the money that we give. Pastors and seminaries, rightly, view generosity as central to our faith, but yet they most often act as if how we earn profits and invest money is something that our faith has little to say about.

If asked to apply a biblical perspective to money and investing, most Christians wouldn't be able to do much more than quote a few Bible verses. We act as if finance exists in a moral vacuum. What this means is our faith is kept from influencing real-life financial decisions.

The Bible frequently warns of the dangers of a "worldly" perspective, by which it means a pattern that we are being squeezed and conformed into by our culture. We are taught that there are boundaries, barriers, and spheres of life completely off-limits to "personal beliefs."

Nancy Pearcy, in her book *Total Truth*, surmises that Christians have mimicked the world in adopting a worldview with two levels which she calls the fact/value split.[8] The upper level is comprised of values which are subjective personal preferences while the lower level contains facts that are binding on everyone.

According to this viewpoint, "values" are synonymous with private tastes or preferences. Truth only resides in the realm of scientific facts. Therefore, according to the secular point of view, to label a position as having to do with "values" is to relegate it to the status of mere personal tastes. In a world where moral values are no longer considered truths, we are free to believe whatever we want so long as we treat it as a non-binding personal preference.

Any Christian who seriously considers this view will realize it is incompatible with faith in Jesus. Our faith rises and falls on the historicity of the resurrection. If the resurrection actually happened, it is an empirical fact which undergirds our faith. The implication is that our faith and resulting values are as true as the law of gravity or the earth's rotation.

Yet, most of us unwittingly accept the fact/value split because it is so pervasive that we don't even realize what is happening. It is the air we breathe.

This is very easy to see if you are looking for it. For instance, the typical Christian will acknowledge that all businesses have values which drive their decision-making, but the choice as to whether to include those values in investment decision-making is relegated to the realm of personal preference. Why doesn't every single follower of Jesus integrate values with investment decision-making? The short answer is that most assume that values are in one realm and the scientific truth of economics resides in a completely different realm and that the two worlds do not intersect.

This could not be further from the truth. In reality, there is only one, whole truth and to the extent something is true, it will have a clear, discernable, and measurable impact. Those companies whose practices, methods, and values are at odds with the chief concerns of our Creator God - those actively working against God's plans to redeem the world - are destined to fail. Maybe not tomorrow. Maybe not next month or next year. But, over the long term, destructive companies will not sustain.

Overcoming the fact/value split means incorporating values into investment decisions not only because it is the right thing to do, but also because it is the prudent and wise thing to do.

CHAPTER 4

Just a Nice Theory?

The Christian financial guru Dave Ramsey hosts one of the most popular radio shows in the nation with more than eight million listeners every week. Ramsey and his company have a very clearly stated position pertaining to values-based investing: *"Dave does not use a values-based investing approach."*

Here's part of the rationale for it: [9]

> *"In values-based investing, you pick between two similar mutual funds that align with your beliefs--a good concept. However, few of these funds stand up to Dave's criteria for picking mutual funds (five-year or longer track record of strong rates of return, professionally managed by a team of mutual funds managers, etc.)"*

He's making the case that screening investments on the basis of values leads to underperformance. The implication of Ramsey's stance here is a reflection of the fact/value dichotomy applied to investing. It is the idea that being concerned about social or moral issues is "touchy-feely" or mushy sentimentality which has no place in the cold harsh world of Wall Street investments.

There is a lot of recent data and statistics which prove this to be false. A recent study from the Wharton School of Business concluded the following: [10]

> *"The overwhelming finding is that incorporating values into investing has a slight positive relationship to performance. What is more important is this dispels the common perception that investing with values comes at the expense of pure financial returns."*

This finding is consistent with a lot of other research. Since 1990, the Social Index (MSCI KLD 400) has outperformed the broad market (S&P 500) by more than half a percent per year (10.46% vs. 9.93%).[11] Mercer Research reviewed 36 different studies on this topic and found that more than half of them (55.6%) showed a definitively positive relationship between performance and values-based investment screens. Less than 10% of those studies showed a clear negative correlation between values-based investment screens and performance.[12]

A Morgan Stanley report from 2015 concluded that *"investing in sustainability has usually met, and often exceeded, the performance of comparable traditional investments."* The research included the performance of 10,228 U.S. mutual funds over seven years. The results showed that returns of "sustainable funds" (a term used for various types of funds using social, environmental, and values-based screening criteria) were equal to or higher than traditional funds 64% of the time. In addition, it found that the sustainable funds averaged lower levels of volatility than the traditional funds.[13]

The second part of Ramsey's rationale for dismissing a values-based approach to investing is as follows:

> *"This is a very personal decision you will have to make. It's what is known as a slippery slope. If you no longer invest in funds that might invest in a company that supports abortion, to be consistent, you will need to stop shopping at the grocer that sells pornography. You would also need to stop banking because nearly all banks contribute to United Way, which supports Planned Parenthood. Do not choose these funds out of guilt. Do not make poor investment decisions to choose these funds."*

The last sentence again poses this false dichotomy between successful investing on the one hand and caring about the moral integrity of the companies being purchased on the other. It is stated as if the two are mutually exclusive and that the de-facto result of integrating values into your investing methodology is "poor investment decisions." It also implies that the only possible motivator for doing so is guilt.

Part of the reason for the explosion in growth of values-oriented investments is due to aforementioned research that consistently shows a positive correlation between investment returns and ethical screens. Far from being driven by "guilt," many investors have found that the best long term bets are those companies that have the most integrity in terms of their mission, culture, and sense of corporate responsibility.

Of course, this should be what we'd expect. If all truth has tangible bearing on reality, then social and moral factors ("values") have a measurable impact on financial performance ("facts"). Morally responsible companies should experience measurable advantages in long term performance either in the form of lower risk or higher returns.

Here are two more subjective reasons why a values-based approach will lead to selecting better long term investments:

First is the connection between competitive advantage and social issues. There are numerous ways in which addressing societal concerns can yield productivity benefits to a company. Consider, for example, what happens when a firm invests in a wellness program. Society benefits because employees and their families become healthier, and the firm minimizes employee absences and lost productivity.

Second, the success of a company is also inextricably linked to the success and sustainability of the communities in which they operate. Ultimately, brand and reputation are more important than ever. Warren Buffett once said it takes a lifetime to build a reputation and five minutes to destroy it. That has never been more true than it is today in the social media age where a company can very quickly ruin its reputation once its morally irresponsible decisions become known. The smartest long term investment strategy is to find those companies that create great value for their customers and constituents.

CHAPTER 5

Slippery Slopes

R amsey's other point is that this is a "slippery slope." Where do you draw the line with a values-based approach to investing in a broken and fallen world? Is the whole attempt to do so futile?

Here's that part of the argument again: *"If you no longer invest in funds that might invest in a company that supports abortion, to be consistent, you will need to stop shopping at the grocer that sells pornography."* Is that true? Should patronage be held to the same standard as ownership? I don't think so.

The person who walks into a convenience store to buy a gallon of milk can have a clear conscience, even if the store sells pornography. In fact, the customer in that scenario is encouraging the store owner to sell more milk and less pornography through the purchase decision. On the other hand, an investor (owner) in the business is responsible for all the products of the business, since he profits from all of the products or services sold by the business.

Consider another hypothetical: Is it hypocritical to not invest in objectionable companies but still use their products? For instance, Johnson and Johnson manufactures abortifacients. Is it a problem if you avoid investing in that company, but use its shampoo?

It is easy to blur the lines and draw moral equivalence, but there is an important distinction to be made. By investing in a company you are becoming a part-owner whether that is through a mutual fund or direct purchase of the stock. The decision to own a company should entail a higher level of due diligence and responsibility than the decision to buy a product.

Although a customer is supporting a business broadly, he is only engaging directly in the product being purchased. Becoming a part-owner of a company - and by extension profiting from its activities and enabling the causes it supports - is different than simply utilizing a product when that is the standard of the industry.

In some instances, avoiding both may be the best answer. But it is much more important to avoid becoming a legal owner in a company that is clearly engaged in destructive or exploitative activities. We should not let the perfect be the enemy of the good in such cases. Drawing a line between ownership and consumption is perfectly reasonable.

CHAPTER 6

The One Question Not Being Asked

D ave Ramsey's Financial Peace University is described as *"a biblically based curriculum that teaches people how to handle money God's ways."* Given this mission, it is ironic that the one thing not being considered in Ramsey's investment philosophy is if God's word has anything to say about the topic.*

This begs the question of whether we believe that scripture can and should shape our views about the purpose of investing. Do we believe in the sufficiency of scripture? 2 Timothy 3:16-17 says that *"all scripture is breathed out by God and profitable for teaching, for reproof, for correction, and for training in righteousness"* so that believers *"may be competent, equipped for every good work."*

In other words, these questions pertaining to the nature and purpose of profit are not beyond the scope of the Bible. While there is no simple Bible verse that provides all the answers, by delving deep into scripture, we will find that the Bible actually has a great deal to say about the subject.

Proverbs 10:2 flatly condemns "ill-gotten treasures" or profits gained by wickedness. In Deuteronomy 23:18, God's people are instructed not to *"bring the fee of a prostitute or the wages of a male prostitute into the house of the Lord your God in payment for any vow, for both of these are abhorrent to the Lord your God."*

These verses reveal that the source of the money mattered a great deal to God and the gift would not be accepted if it was originated in a manner that was contrary to God's will.

We see this in the New Testament as well. When Judas Iscariot tried to give back the money he received for betraying Jesus, even the religious leaders who were responsible for killing Jesus would not take it. They knew it was blood money. As a result, they acknowledged that it could not belong to the Temple treasury any longer. They wanted nothing to do with it because they understood it was given in exchange for the blood of the innocent.

To be clear: the prevalent attitude that says it doesn't matter how I make my money as long as I am generous with the proceeds is not Biblical. The prophet Jeremiah (22:13-16) offers a strong challenge to that type of compartmentalized mentality and invokes the need for integrating faith into how money is used by God's people.

> *"Woe to him who builds his house by unrighteousness, and his chambers by injustice; who uses his neighbor's service without wages, and doesn't give him his hire."*

The Bible clearly directs followers of Jesus to profit in a way that is pleasing to him. In a deeply broken world, this is not a simple task; there are no perfect businesses. Yet, it is imperative that we integrate values with investment decision-making.

* *My intent is not to insinuate that Dave Ramsey is some kind of outlier that needs to be singled out. The reason Ramsey is a relevant example is that his thinking is representative of mainstream Christian thoughts about investing.*

CHAPTER 7

Investor Emotions

We just saw that by being indifferent toward our investments, we are compartmentalizing our faith and our financial decision-making. We are also potentially hurting our investment performance by neglecting to screen out investments in companies that are making ethical decisions that could be damaging over the long run.

On the opposite end of the pendulum from apathy is the tendency to view our financial resources as if we are the owners instead of God. According to Psalm 24, the earth and everything in it, belongs to the Lord. When we neglect to view God as the rightful owner of everything that we have, we tend to tighten our grip on our money and, in an effort to exert total control over financial decisions, our money tends to control us. It also can have detrimental effects on our investments.

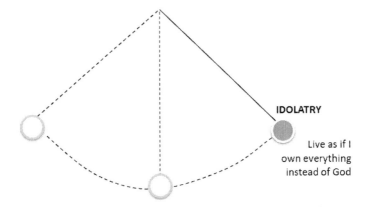

IDOLATRY

Live as if I
own everything
instead of God

According to the latest study from the consulting firm Dalbar, stock fund investors averaged 5.19% per year for the last 20 years as compared to the broad stock market which averaged 9.85%.[14] Many studies have reached similar conclusions. Individual investors tend to greatly underperform due to the tendency to buy shares near market highs and sell shares near market lows. Of course, this is the exact opposite of the key investment mantra to "buy low and sell high."

This investor behavior does not make sense when you look at investing through the lens of rational decision-making. When the markets are low, investments are essentially "on sale" and, therefore, represent the best buying opportunity as opposed to when prices have already gone up.

The problem stems from the fact that very few of us are truly rational in our decision-making, especially when it comes to investing. We all tend to be influenced immensely by our emotions which can lead to horrible financial decisions. The emotional roller coaster chart shown on the next page illustrates how this works.

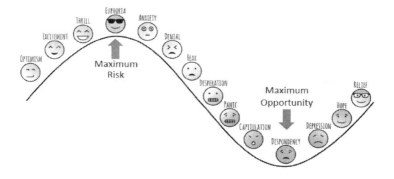

When things are good – the stock market is up, the news headlines are relatively positive, and the economy is expanding – we tend to feel good about investing as well. In other words, we tend to be most "bullish" when prices are at their highest. While we may know in theory that things cannot continue on an upward trajectory indefinitely, greed tends to kick in and we want to participate even more in the upside.

The reverse is also true. As the stock market takes a downturn, our emotions tend to do the same. As headlines grow gloomier, we begin to panic about our investments. Fear is a very influential force and can cause us to sell when we should instead be doing the opposite by rebalancing our investments toward stocks rather than away from them.

CHAPTER 8

The Power of Convictions

In the face of emotions that are detrimental to your wealth, the most common advice is to automate. Have a plan in place and stick to it so that your emotions do not dictate your decision-making. This is advice I have personally recommended.[15]

However, although it is helpful, it does not address the underlying issue. The conventional wisdom assumes that we are all destined to be forever trapped in a cycle of fear and greed, and the best thing we can hope for is to "manage" it. Being resigned to riding an endless emotional roller coaster for the rest of your life does not sound like financial freedom. Rather than just hoping that the seat belt is securely tightened, why not get off the roller coaster altogether?

A fundamental problem for the vast majority of investors (and their advisors) is that they view investing only as a means to an end. When the investments themselves do not ultimately matter, then it is difficult – if not impossible – to have any strong convictions. And it is convictions more than any other single factor that allow us to withstand turbulent market conditions.

To have strong convictions in your investments, it helps to form a connection with the investments you are making. I've worked with many business owners over the years and they do not struggle with convictions. Successful entrepreneurs understand the investments they are making in their businesses; same goes for successful real-estate investors.

They are not tempted to sell at the first hint of a downturn in the market or their industry. Instead, they look to reinvest back into the business or buy on the "dips" because they know and understand these investments. They believe in them.

As long as investments are merely numbers on a page or ticker symbols that are bought and sold on a whim, we cannot form any real convictions about them. But if we treat investing as the sacred responsibility of stewarding God's resources, that will change. If we consider ourselves to be trustees of all that God has entrusted us with, we can simultaneously have a burden that begins to lift now that we no longer "own" everything even as we take the responsibility of investing more seriously.

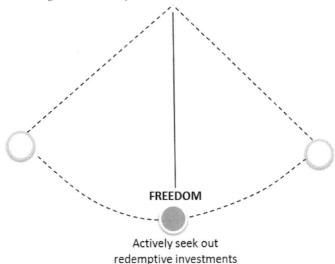

FREEDOM

Actively seek out
redemptive investments

Some people will ask, "What difference does it really make?" You may think that you don't have enough money to worry about this. But whether it is $5 or $5,000,000, the point is not the amount. It is the fact that a conscious choice is being made to make investments that are aligned with – or at a minimum not opposed to – the kingdom of God.

The Parable of the Talents in Matthew 25 emphasizes the importance of small things. Although entrusted with little, the faithful servant is commended for his response. He is not commended because of the amount with which he was entrusted or even for the amount of his increase. It is the quality of being faithful that is most important.

When God commands His people to be set apart and holy, he does not qualify the directive. He does not tell them to be holy in the big things of life or only in the areas where it will make a perceivable difference. Instead, it is a broad imperative with no qualifications attached.

So, now the task turns to implementation. How should we go about integrating faith so that it reflects a distinctive approach toward investing?

CHAPTER 9

The Double-Bottom Line

Traditionally, most people have invested purely in search of profits. If you wanted to make a difference in the community, you would do that through your gifting.

This results in a compartmentalized approach that divides financial intentions into two buckets: one for investing and one for charitable giving. It means you are seeking to achieve a financial return with a classic investing strategy and a social return through philanthropy.

Financial Return

Classic Investing

Social Return

Philanthropy

The problem with this approach is that it ignores a fundamental reality. All businesses have a social return. The only question is whether it is a positive or negative one. Are the underlying companies you invest in – through stocks, bonds, and mutual funds - creating value or extracting value?

Perhaps the easiest way to understand the problem with a compartmentalized approach toward investing is to consider the example of charitable accounts. Even if you don't have a charitable account (i.e., a charitable trust, donor advised fund, private foundation, etc.), imagine a pool of money that is set aside for gifting purposes in which 5% of the balance is given away to charitable causes every year. The key question to consider is "what about the other 95%?"

In other words, what types of companies and business practices are you supporting through your direct investments within that charitable account? Are the underlying investments aligned with the causes you are supporting with your gifting?

If you don't intentionally incorporate some sort of social values screen, it is almost certain you own companies that are actually undermining the causes you are supporting with your gifting. Here are a few hypothetical examples:

- Gifting to organizations that promote the well-being of disadvantaged children while investing in tobacco companies that are actively promoting the sale of an addictive drug to young children in developing countries.
- Gifting to causes concerned with environmental conservation and sustainable farming practices while investing in companies that derive profits from agribusiness, pesticides, and fast food.
- Gifting to crisis pregnancy centers and adoption agencies while investing in companies that give money to Planned

Parenthood and others that profit directly from abortion-related products and services.

It is not difficult to imagine many, many more examples. The solution is to redefine "the bottom line" you are trying to achieve with investing. If you are no longer singularly concerned with financial returns but also social returns, then you are taking a "double-bottom line" approach toward investing and magnifying the social impact on the causes you care about.

Approximately 75% of investors under age 40 now say the social and environmental impact of the companies they invest in is important to their decision-making. The same is true for 45% of investors age 60 or older.[16] This is a positive trend, and the question for us is: As followers of Jesus, how should we think about investing?

There should be two primary investment objectives beyond the traditional goals of maximizing return and minimizing risk:

1) Do No Harm – Avoid investments in companies whose actions and priorities are in conflict with the Kingdom of God

2) Do Good – Actively seek out investments in companies that are helping to redeem a broken world

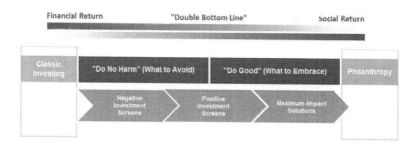

Investing is a sacred responsibility. In order to be faithful to our beliefs, it is incumbent upon us as Christians to take a double bottom line approach toward investing which integrates values into the investment selection process.

CHAPTER 10

Do No Harm

As followers of Jesus, we can and should agree on one basic premise. We are all created in the image of God. However fallen or lost we may be, there is inherent worth – indeed, eternal worth – in each of us. There is dignity and value to each human life. As a Christian, there cannot be debate over this fundamental point.

There are more than 2,000 verses in the Bible that address the poor, the oppressed, and the marginalized. It is a Biblical mandate to prioritize serving the interests of those who are powerless to serve their own interests.

From the modern day slave trade to abortion to the pornography industry, human beings created in the image of God are being dehumanized and commoditized. They are treated as merchandise which can be sold, exchanged, or discarded. It is not coincidental that Christ was betrayed for thirty pieces of silver. The Son of God himself was treated as a piece of merchandise. We are supposed to see this and understand its implications in a modern setting.

Money is an extremely powerful force and the question that every one of us should ask is: Am I aware of the causes my money is supporting? A typical mutual fund may hold anywhere from twenty to five hundred companies. What are those companies doing? How are they profiting and, in return, how are you profiting as a shareholder?

In the past, there have been legitimate limitations in terms of the number of choices available in order to implement such a strategy but that has changed. There are now a significant number of funds that facilitate a values-based approach to investing according to what is known as Biblically Responsible Investing (BRI) or faith-based investing. These are mutual fund companies that screen out stocks which profit from or support abortion, pornography, and tobacco, among other industries.

The Christian Investment Forum is a good place to find an introduction to this topic. John Siverling, Executive Director of the Christian Investment Forum, explains the substantial growth in faith-based investing: [17]

> *"15 years ago there were no more than 5 mutual funds that described themselves as BRI focused. Today, there are at least 100 different mutual funds across 28 different categories that explicitly incorporate Christian faith values as part of their investment process."*

While there are different filters being used to screen out certain stocks, there is a common effort among BRI funds to avoid investing in companies that contribute to the destruction or diminishment of human life.

In defense of the lives of unborn image-bearers of God, our response to this should be direct and intentional. Instead of investing in mutual funds, stocks, or bonds in search solely of maximizing investment returns, add a simple screen. Avoid investing in companies that profit from abortion or provide charitable dollars to support organizations that provide abortions.

Imagine the cumulative and enduring impact that could be made if millions of Christ-followers were simply intentional about their investments in this way. Based on research about those who identify as Christians and claim an interest in aligning investments with their faith, it is estimated that the market size for faith-based investing could be as high as $7 trillion. [18] Given the power of money in our culture, a broad pro-life investing trend would send a strong message and, undoubtedly, impact corporate decision-making.

Christians should no longer blindly invest as everyone else does because we will be unwittingly supporting causes that are in direct opposition to God's kingdom. Living with integrity means aligning our investments with our beliefs. And now that there are investment options that provide legitimate alternatives, we can invest accordingly.

CHAPTER 11

Do Good

Tim Weinhold, Director of Faith & Business at Eventide Funds, says *"We must be careful not to support and foster (and become shareholder owners of) companies who work against human flourishing, who extract rather than create value."* [19]

This is, of course, in line with the "do no harm" philosophy but he takes it a step further and offers this proactive vision for what he calls Biblically-wise investing:

> *"The overarching objective, the guiding purpose, must be to support and foster those companies whose products and practices create real value for others, i.e., companies who are making a consequential contribution to human flourishing."*

It is helpful to think of parallels to the medical industry. Physicians take an oath to "do no harm." It is fundamental to the practice of medicine. But the goal is certainly not to stop there. The ultimate goal of medicine is to heal. Likewise, we should not merely seek to avoid companies doing harm, but ultimately look for companies that heal; those that are helping to make the world a better place.

If we are to take the words of Jesus seriously, loving our neighbor should be the overarching objective. Yet, when we think about the implications of being a healing force for good, there are practical limitations for what that means. In business, there are tradeoffs and a need to prioritize competing objectives.

For example, a company considering whether to outsource jobs may be weighing a positive impact on the company's long term sustainability with a negative impact on its employees. It may force an ethical dilemma that must be addressed: Are the jobs provided for the local community more important than jobs created for those on the other side of the world? What if the positions are outsourced to India and they are still paid a fair (albeit lower) wage which is essentially equal relative to the different standards of living?

Whose well-being should be prioritized? Is our instinct in these situations more about patriotism (to support the local community and its employees) than about the gospel (to love all of God's image-bearers)? Or are there other decision-making filters to apply?

Beyond the soundbites or what feels good, how does a follower of Jesus make such decisions? It all comes down to a central question. Who is our "neighbor"? And, in turn, what does it look like for us to be a neighbor as Christ defined it?

When Jesus is asked this question (in Luke 10:25-37), he tells the story of the Good Samaritan, in which three individuals encounter a man on the side of the road who had just been robbed, beaten, and left for dead. The first two observers – a Priest and a Levite – both neglected to help the man as they passed on the other side of the road. The third person – a Samaritan – came to the man and "took pity on him." He bandaged his wounds, found him shelter, and paid for it on his behalf.

After telling his parable, Jesus asked:

"Which of these three do you think was a neighbor to the man who fell into the hands of robbers?"

When the listener answered that it was the Samaritan who had mercy, Jesus instructs him to "go and do likewise."

The most common interpretation of the parable is that a neighbor is anyone in need. Since we have no reason to believe that these three men – the Priest, the Levite, or the Samaritan – knew the injured man, the implication is that anyone can be our neighbor. But just because anyone can become our neighbor (future state) does not mean that everyone is our neighbor (currently).

It is important to note that Jesus does not refute the premise of the question. When asked to define neighbor, he doesn't say that we are to make no distinction between neighbors and strangers. If that were case, there would have been no need for Jesus himself to invoke the term "neighbor" in the preceding verse. He could have simply instructed that we are to love all people.

The operative question here is why the Samaritan and the wounded man who were strangers just moments prior are now deemed to be neighbors? What changed for all of these characters in the story?

They had an encounter. Their lives intersected.

The man on the side of the road is no longer a stranger because he is in a situation of pressing need and they each have the capacity to respond and are in a position to help. In short, there are two prerequisites for being considered a neighbor: 1) an addressable need and 2) proximity.

Of course, the challenge is to translate these principles into a workable framework for evaluating businesses as potential investment opportunities. More than any other firm in the financial industry, Eventide Funds has contemplated this issue and, in response, developed what they call their "Business 360 Assessment."

The idea is that companies impact six different constituencies or stakeholders: Customers, Employees, Supply Chain, Communities, Environment, and Society. Eventide asserts that this combination of stakeholders allows us to understand the true nature of a company's impact in terms of the good or harm it is doing. Its Business 360 helps answer the question: Is this business creating value or extracting value in terms of the well-being of its employees? Customers? Suppliers? What about the impact on the local community, the environment, or society at large?

It is important to note that not all six constituencies are weighted equally. Since proximity is central to defining the term neighbor, those stakeholders closest to the business should have the greatest weighting. For example, a company's impact on society at large is important, but not quite as important as its impact on its customers or its employees. A business has a direct and immediate impact on its employees and customers in a way it does not have on the overall society or local community in which it operates. All are important and should be taken into account, but not all in equal proportion

A final point in understanding the parable is that Jesus is flipping the question around when he asks "who was the neighbor?" He is redirecting the attention of the hearer from the wounded man on the side of the road to the one of the three passersby who acted as a neighbor to him.

Jesus is saying the primary question is what type of people we are going to be. From an investing standpoint, are we going to support businesses that – like the Good Samaritan – are helping to bring about justice and healing? Are we actively seeking to financially support those businesses that are bringing about human flourishing through the various ways they affect their different constituencies?

The great thing about the Business 360 framework is that it allows us to not only identify companies to avoid, but also it provides a methodology for actively seeking out redemptive investments. It helps us to interpret what it means to love our neighbor. Jesus taught us that what matters most is who *we* are and that is revealed by what we do with our money.

The visual illustration on page 77 showed how - in addition to doing no harm through our investing - we are aiming to do good by intentionally looking to invest in those companies creating great value and positive social impact on the constituencies they serve.

This is often known as "impact investing." So, let's consider a few real life examples of the types of businesses which might make good candidates, given this investment philosophy.

CHAPTER 12

Missionary vs. Mercenary

John Doerr is a partner at Kleiner, Perkins, Caufield & Byers, who made early investments in enormously successful companies like Genentech, Google, and Amazon. The most critical distinction he looks for in a new investment is a "high impact entrepreneur." He says it is ultimately *less about what they do and more about what they believe and how they behave.* He describes the entrepreneurs he most wants to invest in as "missionaries." He contrasts them with less desirable entrepreneurs he calls "mercenaries."

In a speech at Stanford Business School, Doerr described mercenaries as being opportunistic and "all about the pitch and the deal" concerned primarily with short-term payoffs. Missionaries, on the other hand, are more strategic and are concerned with the big idea. He described mercenaries as having "a lust for making money" and missionaries as having "a lust for making meaning." While mercenaries fret over "financial statements," missionaries obsess about "values statements." [20]

John D'Eri is a missionary entrepreneur. He has launched a number of successful businesses, and his most recent one is a car wash in Florida. It may not sound like much at first glance, but it is creating a legion of advocates. Customers are consistently asking for flyers to hand out because they love its mission.

Rising Tide Car Wash was founded in Parkland, Florida in 2013, and today it employs 35 autistic men and women. John D'Eri's son, Andrew, was one of his father's first hires at the car wash. He is in his early 20's and autistic. So D'Eri is very familiar with the struggles that those with autism face. Somewhere between 65% and 90% of people with autism are unemployed or underemployed. Over the next decade, at least another 500,000 people with autism will enter the workforce so figuring out a way to gainfully employ them will become increasingly important.

Rising Tide tracks employee growth with surveys, given to both employees and their families. What they have found is that their autistic employees have experienced significant improvements in confidence and social skills. Perhaps the most important contributor to their overall well-being is the pride regarding the work they do and the friendships they have developed. Tom D'Eri is Andrew's older brother and co-owner of the car wash with his father. This is how he described the impact on autistic people who they have employed: [21]

> *"They come to us with very little purpose and very little hope for their future. But once they start working with us they start getting positive reinforcement of doing a good job, a customer being happy, getting a tip, that really starts to open them up."*

Crucial to this story is the fact that John and Tom D'Eri did not just start a business and decide to hire people with autism as a charitable act. They spent a significant amount of time researching various opportunities and identified the car wash industry as potentially the best match for those with autism since they are more likely to thrive in an environment with the types of detailed, repetitive processes required.

All businesses are desperate to find a competitive advantage. Rising Tide aims to build its competitive advantage by leveraging the unique talents of individuals with autism in order to become the premium brand in the car wash industry. Individuals with autism are typically really good with structured tasks, following processes, and attention to detail. These are important attributes for an industry that is so dependent on repetitive service done consistently well.

This is how Rising Tide Car Wash articulates its mission:

> "By delivering a first-rate car wash experience to the consumer, Rising Tide strives to inspire communities to change their perception of the capabilities of people with autism."

Rising Tide is a for-profit business and intending to franchise its model in the near future. There have never been federal or state grants or any subsidies involved in the founding or continuation of operations. This is just one example that debunks the myth that we have to either choose to do social good or choose to make profits. There need not be a drag on profitability if a business intelligently incorporates a social component to it. If done well, it results in a more profitable business model with inherent competitive advantages and more loyal customers.

Speaking of profitable business models and loyal customers... Southwest Airlines is by far the most successful company in the airline industry. Herb Kelleher founded the company more than 40 years ago. At that time, there were immensely high costs associated with air travel. As a result, only 15% of the American public had ever flown at that time, since no one but the upper class could afford to fly.

So, Kelleher started Southwest with a very basic but powerful purpose. He wanted to "democratize the skies" by giving people "the freedom to fly." It is no coincidence that, since the time Southwest airlines was founded; the percentage of Americans who have flown has grown from 15% to over 85%.[22]

In order to achieve the purpose of his company, Kelleher has maintained a laser like focus on reducing the price of flying. In order to do that, his company had to completely rethink the prevailing economic model of the airline industry. Among other ideas, Southwest has established a point-to-point system rather than the less efficient hub and spoke model.

Southwest's corporate culture is also unique. The company makes it clear in their values statement that they prioritize employees above all, even customer satisfaction. In order of importance, Southwest ranks employees first, customers second, and shareholders third. *"We believe that if we treat our employees right, they will treat our customers right, and in turn that results in increased business and profits that make everyone happy."* [23]

Each month the Southwest Spirit magazine features the story of an employee who has gone above and beyond. Southwest highlights positive behaviors through a variety of recognition programs and awards.

This employee first culture is also evidenced by their guarantee that employees as well as their spouses, dependent children, and parents all fly for free on Southwest. They've also made deals with other companies that help discount the cost of hotels, theme parks, and rental car companies for their staff.

The end result of all of this focus on mission and corporate values has been Southwest's recognition as one of the world's most admired companies, one of the best companies to work for, and consistently top rankings in customer satisfaction.

CHAPTER 13

Community Development

Praxis Mutual Funds is a faith-based investment fund family that is part of Everence Capital Management. Over the years, Praxis has consistently made investments in community development across the world. By partnering with the Calvert Foundation, they have helped small business owners succeed by lending them capital they would otherwise not be able to access.

Arely Pavon-Torres built a thriving plant business from her home in Xochimilco, Mexico, thanks to access to financial services provided by Praxis' support of a nonprofit women's development organization in Latin America. [24]

In addition to economic empowerment for women business owners, Praxis has also helped fund a number of environmental projects in developing countries. Here are just two examples of bond investments made by the Praxis International Income Fund:

$2.2 million in U.S. Agency for International Development bonds designated for water and wastewater systems in Egypt.

$2 million for the issue of International Finance Facility for Immunization bonds which funded a program to help save millions of children from preventable diseases.

Mark Regier, the V.P. of Stewardship Investing for Praxis, put it this way, in talking about faith-based investment firms as a whole: [25]

> *"They will continue to explore how their portfolios can be more just, more creatively inclusive, more socially impactful, and more values-aligned while remaining true to their financial fiduciary responsibilities and commitments."*

Newmont Mining Corporation is a publicly-traded, multinational corporation that produces gold. A key component of the company's corporate policy is to prioritize community investments as a way to "catalyze long-term socio-economic development."

Prior to initiating commercial development in a new region, Newmont closely engages with local communities to meet their needs through a combination of direct investments in community infrastructure and social programs.

For example, in the process of developing four new mining areas in Ghana in 2006, Newmont compensated roughly 1,700 households located in the region and, in resettling these people, they built new homes and schools, granted them legal title to the land, and provided potable water and access to electricity. As a result, the living conditions for residents of the region were significantly improved.

Newmont even launched a fund to contribute approximately $500,000 annually to support community development programs such as the provision of water, sanitation, upgrading local clinics and training centers. They also provided HIV/AIDS programs for workers as well as a program on malaria prevention, and an information forum for women in the community.

CHAPTER 14

The Greatest Commandment (for Investing)

J esus said the greatest commandment is to *"Love the Lord your God with all your heart and with all your soul and with all your strength and with all your mind; and Love your neighbor as yourself"* (Luke 10:26-27).

In terms of what we do with our money, what are the implications of those words for us? What does loving God with every part of our being, including our money, look like?

We have a choice. We can further shalom or we can further the effects of the fall. And our response should be motivated by enthusiasm rather than guilt. In some small way, we have the opportunity to take part in the kingdom of God breaking through the brokenness in this world.

Anyone who works with a financial advisor knows about a "performance review." Generally, it involves assessing the rates of return of your investments and comparing them with some esoteric market indices (i.e., S&P 500 Index, Barclays Aggregate Bond Index, etc.).   Ideally, it will also focus on how your investment performance affected your ability to achieve your financial goals.

Now, imagine what a performance review *could* look like if investments are viewed not merely as a means to end. What if your investments are no longer statistics on a page or a rather meaningless collage of ticker symbols? What if those investments really meant something? To be sure, the review would still involve a recap of financial returns, but it would be much more than that.

The "social returns" would also be reviewed. How many people with autism were hired by the companies you own? How many fresh water wells were built in developing nations? How many millions of children's lives were saved thanks to the funding of immunizations? How many entrepreneurs in Uganda or Kenya were able to start their own businesses thanks to your investments that help to fund them? How many companies that profit from abortion did you "veto" with your investment dollars? How many tobacco companies peddling addiction to toddlers in developing countries did you screen out?

CHAPTER 15

A Hope-Based Approach

Effective financial management is holistic, which means it is comprehensive in scope and the components are interdependent. Cash flow, taxes, retirement planning, investments, and debt management all impact each other. You cannot make wise financial decisions in a vacuum. Like pieces of a puzzle that fit together in a particular way to form a complete picture, financial decisions are interrelated and contingent on one another.

Many are familiar with the puzzle analogy. But all too often something is missing from it. In order to best put together the puzzle, you need to see the picture on the top of the box. It's tempting to jump right in and begin fitting the pieces together. But you'll have greater success if you understand what it is you are trying to build and confirm it's something you want to build. Likewise, you cannot make the best financial decisions for your life until you have really articulated and envisioned your ideal future — the "picture on the top of the box."

But there is another reason why the "picture" is so portant. Your desired future not only informs decision-making today, but it also provides the incentive to make it a reality. A compelling vision of your desired future will provide the proper motivation for making the right financial decisions. We should envision an ideal "end" and work backwards from there.

For Christians, the need to begin with the end in mind is even more important because our "end" is eternal in nature. That's why, in the New Testament, many of the references to money are framed in terms of ultimate consequences – from rewards in heaven (Matthew 6:2-4) to being cut off from God forever (Matthew 6:19-24). Scripture works from the premise that what we believe about our ultimate future profoundly affects how we approach personal financial matters. If we do not fully contemplate or understand the eternal, we become experts in the trivial and novices in the significant.

So the central question is: what do we believe about our ultimate future and the future of this world? What we believe about heaven and the Kingdom of God is not merely a speculative exercise or obscure theological debate. It informs our daily actions and decision-making.

If I believe that this earth is ultimately going to burn up and be destroyed and my vision of heaven is an ethereal, purely spiritual existence, what I do here doesn't matter much. It matters in terms of saving souls, but none of the work I do or monetary investments I make have a lasting impact. In this view, what matters most is not being "left behind." This often results in Christians becoming "too heavenly minded for any earthly good."

But what we see in Genesis 2:5-15 is that God created us to work. The Garden of Eden is God's vision for humanity and it will ultimately come about. According to the Apostle Paul in 1 Corinthians 15:58, this means that what we do on earth is not in vain. When we know what our eternal future will look like, it will infuse our activities here with a whole new level of meaning and significance.

So how does this all play out on a daily basis in our money relationships? On a practical level, how do these beliefs shape our perspectives and decision-making?

An underdeveloped view of the end of time will lead to a compartmentalized view of personal finances, one that happens to look an awful lot like that of non-believers. In this view:

> I will negotiate the best deal possible, even if it means taking advantage of someone in a tough spot or another person's naivety.

> I will buy the cheapest products and services without considering the supply chain or labor practices that helped produce it.

> I will invest money solely in pursuit of maximized financial returns, regardless of how the companies I am investing in make their profits.

> I will maximize financial wealth without much thought of the potential dangers money may pose to my own soul.

If, on the other hand, we believe God is in the business of restoring every inch of his Creation, as servants in His Kingdom our bottom line is no longer purely financial but rather about serving the greater good with our time, talent, and money. It means we spend money, invest money, and earn money all in ways that are intended to increase human flourishing. We will aspire to use our resources in ways that are beautiful and transformational.

In this view:

I will voluntarily pay more than necessary for some products in order to promote generous labor practices or sustainable agriculture.

I will integrate my values with my investment decisions, avoiding investments in companies that promote the diminishment or destruction of human life.

I will lavishly give my money in ways that are shocking and overflowing with grace.

I will take seriously Jesus's warning that we cannot serve two masters (God and "mammon") by being concerned not only with what I am doing with money but also with what money is doing to me.

Everyone should have a "goal-based" approach to managing money. It's the right framework for making good financial decisions. The difference for followers of Christ is that our greatest goals and dreams are aligned with God's plan for eternity. What we need is a hope-based approach to money. Not a hope in money that rescues us from uncertainty about the future, but a hope that rests assured in the promises of the one who conquered death.

Section III

Third Money Question:

What Is It Doing To You?

(The Importance of Giving & GENEROSITY)

CHAPTER 1

High Expectations

Recently I was doing a financial educational presentation for NBA players. I opened my talk by asking these players to think back to when they signed their first contract. What was their first reaction when they found out how much money they'd be making? I asked them what they recalled about the feeling they had at that point. Joy? Elation? Disbelief? Then I asked about the one answer no one was giving: Fear? Anyone…?

I told them that I don't know what it feels like to have hundreds of people looking to me for help – friends, family members, lots of people who are in real financial need – who are all wanting help to solve those problems. And while I don't personally know what that feels like, I know those are some high expectations placed on you. In fact, in many cases, they are impossible expectations.

It's true that money can help solve some problems, but invariably it is not enough. There is never enough of it to appease people's expectations. And, instead of gratitude toward you, in some cases the people closest to you become resentful and only want more of

103

your money. This is all well-documented in the experiences of legions of former professional athletes.

I shared that with them not because I am advocating for a fearful attitude, but rather so that we could actually talk about the negative repercussions of wealth. It's healthy to counterbalance the messaging all around us that claims that money will bring nothing but happiness.

The fact is money has a potentially corrosive effect not only on our relationships, but ultimately, on our souls. In his parable of the sower, Jesus referred to four different scenarios involving seeds in order to illustrate the different ways we hear God's word: 1) ones that fell on the road and were eaten by birds 2) ones that were planted in shallow soil 3) ones that started to grow but were choked by thorn bushes and 4) ones that were planted in good soil. Regarding those that fell among the thorn bushes, Jesus gave this explanation:

> *"As for what fell among the thorns, these are the ones who hear; but as they go on their way, they are choked by the cares and riches and pleasures of life, and their fruit does not mature."* - Luke 8:14

The seeds that he mentions actually sprout and begin to grow, but the thorns ultimately choke them and smother their new life. As Jesus points out, it is the "cares and riches and pleasures" which act as thorns. It should not be hard for those of us living in the most prosperous nation in the history of the world to see the many ways in which our financial resources can distract and divert us from a focus on God's kingdom.

CHAPTER 2

Seeking Riches

In 1966, 42% of college freshmen said that becoming rich was an important life goal. That figure had increased to 74% by 1990.[1] In a Pew Research Center poll released in 2007, 81% of 18-25 year olds said getting rich is either their first or second most important life goal. (By way of comparison, 30% of those surveyed said the same about helping people who need help. Only ten percent said becoming more spiritual was one of the first or second most important life goals.) [2]

So the bottom line is that earning lots of money is a big priority for people. We worry about how to earn more money, about losing the money we have, and about not running out of money. But we don't much worry about the effect that money is having on us. Most of us tend to feel like we are self-reliant and in control of financial matters. If the potential danger of riches is even a concern at all, it seems to be a rather insignificant and fleeting one for most people.

105

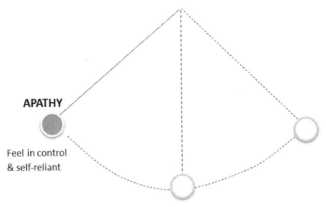

APATHY

Feel in control
& self-reliant

The New Testament in general - and Jesus in particular - talks a lot about money and in ways that should give us pause. Jesus said it is easier for a rich man to go through the eye of a needle than to enter the gates of Heaven. He told a rich young ruler that he needed to give away all he had in order to receive eternal life. He warned us that we cannot worship God and "Mammon."

Why don't we fear the Lord and his warnings in this regard? Why do even followers of Jesus treat money and the accumulation of wealth as an unmitigated good thing? There are two primary reasons for this. First, we act as if we are never going to die. Second, we tend to have too high of an opinion of ourselves.

CHAPTER 3

Ignoring Mortality

We live in an increasingly secular culture and are often unaware of how that affects us. One implication is that the messaging all around us practically ignores or dismisses the afterlife altogether.

This has an effect on those of us who follow Christ. It doesn't mean we also are outright rejecting heaven, hell, or eternity. Instead, more of a functional disbelief sets in. We act as if this life is all there is and make decisions accordingly. It's a subtle, gradual effect that tends to erode our consciousness of our own mortality over time. Ernest Becker captured this whole phenomenon beautifully in his book, *The Denial of Death*.

Becker believes that we form "immortality projects" which allow us to feel superior to physical reality. These endeavors help us to be part of something eternal as compared to our physical bodies, and thereby give us a sense that our lives have real purpose, significance, and meaning. For example, these "immortality projects" can take the shape of extreme devotion and advocacy for certain political causes.

Becker argues that, in pursuit of "proving" the superiority of these belief systems, immortality projects are a fundamental driver of human conflict which can take the shape of wars, bigotry, genocide, and racism. [3]

The solution to this innate craving for meaning and transcendence, rather than these arbitrary and fictional projects that we may devise to deny the fact of our own mortality, is to actually focus on our own mortality. Perhaps the single most important piece of financial wisdom you will hear is this: You are going to die. David's prayer in Psalm 39 (verses 4-7) is a plea to God to allow him to truly comprehend his own mortality and the fleeting nature of this life:

> *"O, Lord, make me know my end and what is the measure of my days; let me know how fleeting I am! Behold, you have made my days a few handbreaths, and my lifetime is as nothing before you. Surely all mankind stands as a mere breath!"*

David Brooks, in his fascinating book, *The Road to Character*, contrasts what he calls "resume virtues" with "eulogy virtues." As the name implies "resume virtues" are those attributes and achievements that we want to tout in order to build up our own stature. These are achievements, successes, and character traits involving things like work ethic, accountability, communication, and leadership. Resume virtues are about accomplishments, performance, and abilities. [4]

Brooks argues that these resume virtues are what we seek after the vast majority of our lives. And yet, they do not reflect what is most important to us. He says our most valued, most treasured qualities and virtues are revealed in our eulogies. When we are honoring the lives of those who have passed away, we don't talk much about how much money they have amassed or how many promotions they received. We talk about their empathy, compassion, and love for others. We talk about how they served and cared for those who were in need. We talk about how they lived as fathers, mothers, children, or friends.

These "eulogy virtues" are what we tend to miss amidst the onslaught of distractions in a highly materialistic culture. This prioritization of the near term over the eternal leads to skewed priorities and disordered loves. Peggy Noonan, speechwriter for President Reagan, may have said it best: [5]

> "In a way, the world is a great liar. It shows you it worships and admires money, but at the end of the day it doesn't. It says it adores fame and celebrity but it doesn't, not really. The world admires, and wants to hold on to, and not lose, goodness. It admires virtue... That's what it really admires. That's what we talk about in eulogies, because that's what's important. We don't say, 'The thing about Joe was he was rich.' We say, if we can, 'The thing about Joe was he took care of people.'"

There are things that no one says when they are lying on their deathbeds: "I wish I had made more money." "I'm so glad for the size of my portfolio." In that moment, what matters is really clear. It's all about relationships – loving God and loving others. It's at that moment when the Greatest Commandment is first and foremost in people's minds. It all begs the question, of course, why should we wait until we're on our deathbeds to inevitably figure that out?

CHAPTER 4

Thinking Too Highly of Ourselves

A nother reason we don't fear the Lord or heed the many scriptural warnings about money is because we have too high of an opinion of ourselves. Brooks examined how self-perception has experienced a sea change over the last two generations and explained that people in the first half of the 20th century were much more skeptical and distrustful of their own instincts. They didn't automatically prize being "true to themselves" because of concern that their instincts and desires may often be sinful or misguided.

This formerly cautious attitude toward our personal desires has been undermined by our current culture which constantly promotes high self-esteem and self-actualization. This is not all bad. Certainly, women and minority groups in particular have been the benefactors of a greater sense of personal worth and confidence. And many people have done great things and utilized God-given talents much more fully instead of being held back by fear and self-doubt as a result.

But the constant knee-jerk celebration of being true to oneself is potentially very harmful if we believe we are ultimately sinners in desperate need of God's grace. As followers of Jesus, we *should* question our motives, desires, and instincts. And we should have legitimate concerns about the effects money may have on us. We should distrust our instinctive abilities to handle money in ways that glorify God.

If we were more reflexively skeptical of our own tendencies and emotions rather than blindly trusting of them, we would be much more apt to heed Christ's many warnings about money and its corrupting influence on our souls. As it is now, we tend to view these passages of scripture as messages for other people. "I don't struggle with greed, but my neighbor could really benefit from this message."

Also, we relativize the message and minimize its effects. "Jesus is not really saying give away everything; it's just a way of making a point." We make sure to point out that the apostle Paul did not say that money itself is the root of all evil, but rather the love of money. This is true, of course, but we should be leery of acting as if that simple clarification is a huge relief. In a consumer culture where the average person is exposed to at least 3,000 ads per day, there is surely plenty of money loving to go round.

CHAPTER 5

The Right Kind of Fear

he creator of the universe is an all loving and all powerful God who is a father to us and has told us not to fear what we wear or what we will eat. Still we struggle with fear. If we are going to fear - if that is inevitable - we should fear appropriately. There is one fear that is legitimate and that is the fear of God. There is a 100% chance we will die and someday sit in the judgment of our Lord. There is a certain sense of fear that is rational in that regard.

So, which kind of fear will we choose to adhere to: the one that will paralyze us and fill us with anxiety because of some false notion of our own control or independence? Or the one that will determine our eternal fate?

John Newton famously wrote, *"Twas Grace that taught my heart to fear."* The Psalms tell us the fear of the Lord is the beginning of wisdom; that it does so by making us humble. We are not to think of God as a vindictive task master. That is not the way in which the Bible advocates fearing the Lord.

113

Fear of the Lord properly understood was well articulated by Sinclair Ferguson, who called it: *"that indefinable mixture of reverence, fear, pleasure, joy, and awe which fills our hearts when we realize who God is and what He has done for us."* [6]

I have a picture of the coast of the Isle of Capri etched permanently and vividly into my mind. My wife and I almost didn't go to the island off the southwestern coast of Italy. It wasn't in the original itinerary for our Italian excursion, but I'm grateful for the last minute change of plans.

There was something overwhelming about that place. Looking out into the great blue yonder off the coast of the small island, I marveled at the endless horizon. I had never been on an island before, much less one that seemed so remote and pristine, many thousands of miles from anywhere familiar to me. At one point, I was actually overcome by a palpable sense of fear.

I can't explain it really, but there is something unmistakable when you get a glimpse of how immense and spectacular the universe really is. Maybe you know what I mean. As an American, the vast majority of the time, I take for granted a certain sense of comfort, control, and security. When I realized how very small I am and how little control of my fate I actually have, it was humbling and frightening, and yet liberating.

At precisely these moments, it becomes clear to me that far too many of us spend much of our lives in "the fog of the ordinary," feeling that each day is pretty much the same as the last and wishing for something more. We don't see that we are in fact living in the midst of a magnificent creation. This is actually the more accurate way of comprehending reality than an orderly and controlled understanding of life.

Recognizing the world's wonder and fragility — the breathtaking grandeur on offer from the Creator — is seeing reality. Ordinariness, on the other hand, stems from the delusion of self-sufficiency.

To stand in appreciation and astonishment of God's power, beauty, and majesty – to be captivated by wonder and awe – gives us a good sense of what it means to fear God.

Standing at the tip of land's end, where the next body of land was a different continent a thousand miles away, my ego was greatly diminished. Nature has a way of pointing us to this reality. My own "smallness" was unmistakable.

Psalm 8:3-4 speaks of our Creator this way:

> *"When I look at your heavens, the work of your fingers, the moon and the stars, which you have set in place, what is man that you are mindful of him, and the son of man that you care for him?"*

CHAPTER 6

The Vital Importance of What We Love

In Matthew 6:21, Jesus teaches us *"where your treasure is, there your heart will be also."* When the Bible refers to the "heart," it is referring to the control center of your entire being. It is where you put your ultimate hope. The nature of Biblical love is totalitarian: it involves and binds the whole person. That's the reason for the strong love/hate language in the Bible.

Power is never neutral; it orients people. That is why Jesus talked about God and "Mammon" being in conflict. (Mammon is an Aramaic word that usually means money and also can mean wealth.) Jesus is saying that money is not neutral; it has a spiritual power. Mammon can be a master the same way that God is; it is a power that tries to be like God; it makes itself our master and has specific goals.

By examining what is really driving our financial decision-making, we can discover more precisely the nature of our brokenness and what it is we actually love the most.

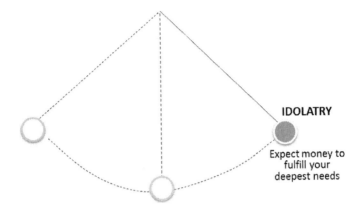

IDOLATRY

Expect money to
fulfill your
deepest needs

"We need instruction on how to possess money without being possessed by money. We need help to learn how to own things without treasuring them."

– Richard Foster [7]

CHAPTER 7

Key Financial Motivators

Initial attempts to diagnose our primary financial motivations will likely yield general observations. For instance, through candid introspection about my own feelings related to money, I may acknowledge a struggle with greed, materialism, or envy. That is helpful but it is not specific enough.

To determine what it is I actually "treasure," I need to dig deeper in order to identify the ultimate driver. Consider the following: "I struggle with greed because I ultimately seek _____ and believe money can provide it." Or "I am envious of people who are richer than me because money can help them experience a greater degree of _____."

Based on both research and personal experience as a financial planner, I believe we can narrow it down to four possible options for filling in those blanks. The primary motivators for financial decisions are 1) control (security) 2) comfort (freedom) 3) power (status) and 4) approval (love). None of these are inherently bad things, of course, but each of us are prone to turn at least one of these into an idol by valuing it above all else and looking for money to provide it.

You can go to redefiningfinancialfreedom.com to take a 5 minute online assessment that will provide you with a diagnosis of your primary financial motivator (i.e., control, comfort, power, or approval).

These financial motivators are not obvious. That's why the Bible cautions us to "watch out!" for greed and monetary temptations (Luke 12:15). We can often be completely oblivious to sinfulness related to money because there are no easily identifiable markers or absolutes (i.e., you know if you've committed adultery, murder, or lied but materialism or greed is a lot harder to identify). It really is a heart issue which may go completely undetected, particularly in a culture that prizes individualism and financial success above all else.

For instance, many highly successful and wealthy people trust in money to provide them security. An undercurrent of worry and anxiety about never having "enough" can actually fuel fiscal responsibility. As a result, this type of person can end up in an admirable financial position in which even most church-sponsored money management courses would provide nothing but positive reinforcement and praise.

Of course, this is not all bad; financially responsible behaviors should be encouraged. But if we are concerned about more than achieving some version of the American dream, we need to examine not only the results but also the motivations fueling those results. In this example, a desire for control may very well be this person's functional savior. Financial independence may provide an illusion of control and self-sufficiency which does not require trust in God for provision.

In Philippians 4:11-12, Paul says

"I have learned in whatever situation I am to be content. I know how to be brought low, and I know how to abound. In any and every circumstance, I have learned the secret of facing plenty and hunger, abundance and need."

In absence of the type of contentment Paul is describing here, we have an unquenchable desire for control and financial security which requires a need for certainty. We will never be able to have this certainty and our need for it undermines our ability to ever be free.

If we delude ourselves into believing we are in control, we can come to expect certain outcomes that we "deserve." The resulting attitude of not getting what is owed to us is often self-pity or resentment.

By contrast, we should seek to embrace uncertainty in circumstances as Paul does. Doing so allows us to experience freedom because we are not owed anything. This is the polar opposite of what is known as the "prosperity gospel," which teaches that if you learn the right words and speak them in faith, you can find your "victory" and be rewarded with material wealth and healing.

In Acts 8:20-24, Simon the magician acts as if God is a power that can be manipulated and bought. Paul does not equivocate in responding to this heresy. His response is direct and forceful when he tells Simon that he and his money can go to Hell. We need to have a similar resolve in recognizing and rebuking the pervasive heresy in evangelical culture that says God will provide material wealth and health to those who have enough faith.

Jacques Ellul, in his book, *Money & Power*, observes: [8]

"We distrust God and place our confidence in things. We prefer our relation to money over our relation to God. This money relationship is ultimately a subordination of what we are to what we have. Being thus entirely turned in on ourselves, we end up alienating ourselves in what we own."

The person who looks to money to provide a certain level of status or image is likely to have an unceasing level of discontent beneath the surface. For this person, there is typically a hunger for power which can become an insatiable desire; like spraying water in the most arid desert lands, you always need more. Any hopes of genuine joy or gratitude from the fruits of financial success often quickly evaporate for this person.

The real problem with this is the perceived self-reliance the Bible is warning against in Deuteronomy 8:17-18:

> *"Beware lest you say in your heart, 'My power and the might of my hand have gotten me this wealth.' You shall remember the Lord your God, for it is he who gives you power to get wealth."*

Those who ultimately seek comfort do not struggle with enjoying the fruits of their labor. They tend to search for experiences and a certain type of freedom. But instead of freedom to become part of God's redemptive mission for the world, they desire freedom from constraints and the pursuit of fleeting pleasures which distracts us from what really matters. This is the truth Jesus was revealing when he told his disciples the following parable in Luke 12:16-21:

> *"The ground of a certain rich man yielded an abundant harvest. He thought to himself, 'What shall I do? I have no place to store my crops.'*
>
> *Then he said, 'This is what I'll do. I will tear down my barns and build bigger ones, and there I will store my surplus grain. And I'll say to myself, "You have plenty of grain laid up for many years. Take life easy; eat, drink and be merry."'*
>
> *But God said to him, 'You fool! This very night your life will be demanded from you. Then who will get what you have prepared for yourself?'"*

The last of the primary money motivators is the need for approval. For this person, net worth equals self-worth. The irony is that the more money that is accumulated, the more insecure she becomes. This can be seen in the mindset of certain inheritors of great wealth. They are constantly questioning the true motives of others. They wonder, "Do people like me as a person (out of genuine love, respect, or admiration) or are they simply being nice to me because of my money?"

What this reveals is a sense of shame or a feeling that I'm not what I ought to be. Research professor Brenee Brown describes shame as *"The intensely painful feeling that we are flawed and therefore unworthy of love and belonging."* [9] These lies of shame deny that we are created in the image of God. It is what we are trying to cover up when we look to money to provide us with love and approval.

Not surprisingly, these hopes that money promises to deliver fail us and, more often than not, the underlying desire actually increases along with the person's balance sheet. Addiction may be the best way to describe the situation. Despite unparalled levels of prosperity in America, we feel trapped by an endless pattern of emotional distress in which the apparent object of our desire only serves to intensify the desire itself. Hence, the debt crisis we face as a nation both at the level of the individual and the federal government.

CHAPTER 8

Shattering the Illusion of Control

S o what is the answer? We cannot hope to simply remove these disproportionate desires. As Augustine might say, we are made to love and what we love defines us. Instead, we need to fall in love with God's kingdom above all else. We need to be motivated by "treasures in heaven," but first we should come to grips with the folly of our assumptions.

I find it helpful to recognize the absurdity of thinking I am in control and self-reliant. When I begin to believe or act as if I am self-sufficient, I will ask myself the following questions:

Do I grow the food I eat?

Do I sew the clothes I wear?

Do I heal my body when I am sick?

Do I write the books that teach my children?

Do I provide water to drink?

Do I build my means of travel - bikes, cars, planes?

Am I responsible for the air I breathe?

Am I responsible for where or when I was born?

Do I control the fact that my children were born into a culture of prosperity rather than poverty?

Should I take credit for these things? Am I living as if I am to thank or God is to thank?

What difference does it make if I am interdependent vs independent? What if all that I have is not my own? Would I be asking a different question about my money? Not "how much of my money should I give away" But "how much of God's money should I keep for myself"?

As long as I maintain the illusion of control and continue to believe that I am independent and self-reliant, I will give begrudgingly out of guilt. But once I can begin to grasp the true nature of reality - how miniscule my contribution and how massive his gifts - I will be awed by his staggering grace and love. I will begin to really embrace the words, "Not my will but thy will be done." I will be so filled with gratitude that I will scheme of ways to give away money.

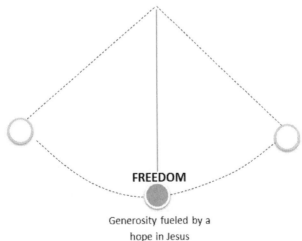

FREEDOM

Generosity fueled by a
hope in Jesus

CHAPTER 9

Overcoming Cynicism

If we can affirm the good in the world, we can begin to truly appreciate what we have. This is not an easy task in a world so focused on the negative. Twenty-four hour news thrives on hyping headlines that provoke fear, anger, and cynicism. Cynicism is a great temptation of modern life. It is so pervasive and commonly accepted that we may even be blinded to it.

For instance, if someone is called a "true believer," that is meant as an insult. Think of how often reviews of movies or music describe something as "irreverent" and mean it as the highest form of praise. We must diligently fight against this cynicism because it makes it much harder to believe in anything. It prevents us from deeply connecting to God and undermines our ability to really experience true meaning and purpose in our lives.

In a recent *Wall Street Journal* editorial, Bret Stephens said it this way: [10]

"We become cynics because we don't want to be moralists, and because earnestness is boring, and because skepticism is a hard and elusive thing to master... Cynicism gives us the comfort of knowing we won't be fooled again because we never believed in anything in the first place."

Our ingenuity, creativity, and freedom are all stifled by cynicism and misplaced fear so we must be aware of competing interests. Politicians and the media alike are self-interested in stoking economic fears and divisions. Not surprisingly, angry rhetoric fills the airwaves with incessant talk about income inequality, big oil, shipping jobs overseas, and illegal immigrants stealing jobs.

Regardless of where you fall on the political spectrum, you are susceptible to the temptations of bitterness, anger, and disgust. Record numbers of people now think the United States is on the wrong track. More people than ever before distrust all authorities and institutions. The quickest way to be ostracized is to side with any sort of "establishment," which may take the shape of government, big business, or traditional religion, to name a few.

We think we are free in our thoughts; our culture tells us the environment is ours to shape and our stories are ours to write. But the fact is we are all far more shaped by our environment than the other way around. And the only way to retain a healthy economic mindset is to push back against the angry drumbeat. Amidst the deep cynicism driving activist movements like Occupy Wall Street that constantly decry the evils of capitalism, it is easy to miss a miraculous system occurring in our midst.

CHAPTER 10

Miracles of a Free Market

I n modern society, we can trust an entire legion of strangers to be ethical and accountable to deliver on promises. Think of any single purchase you make: maybe it's a bag of coffee. Do you feel the need to open it up in the store before you buy it to make sure it's not just filled with dirt or sawdust? When you pump gasoline into your car, how do you know you're not being duped and filling your car with water instead?

The fact is we constantly make purchases like this and take for granted all that is taking place to enable it all to happen. There is a deep ecology of trust based on reciprocity. A manufacturer of goods must keep its word or no retailer will buy from it again. If a retailer wants customers to keep coming back, it must deliver on its promises.

This is increasingly true since the information explosion and prevalence of social media. A largely self-regulating web of businesses and organizations all work together rather seamlessly to meet all our needs and wants. And they deliver it all to our doorstep at the click of a button.

In 1958, Leonard E. Read wrote an essay called "I, Pencil" which we can all learn a lot from nearly 60 years later. He asserts that a single pencil warrants our admiration and awe and that "not a single person on the face of this earth" knows how to make a pencil. He then goes on to enumerate all the different people, skills, and materials involved in producing a pencil.

He starts with the cedar trees in the Pacific Northwest and all the saws, trucks, and rope using in harvesting the logs. He describes what is involved in transporting the logs to a mill which required individuals making flat cars and rails and railroad engines. Then, he proceeds to describe the millwork involved – from the cutting of logs into slats to the tinting and waxing of the exterior of the pencil to all of the work and skill that is required to construct and operate the mill itself.

Moving on to the pencil factory, he explains the eight slats of wood which are finely carved to fit neatly over the lead and all glued together. Then, there is the lead itself and all the mining, tools, and expertise needed to make it. He describes the lacquer coating which provides the yellow sheen and then goes on to elaborate as to how the metal near the end of the pencil is produced. Finally, he concludes by describing the "crowning glory" which is the eraser and its components sourced from the Dutch East Indies and Italy. [11]

Read's point in writing that article was to show that there is no single master mind, dictating and directing the countless actions required in manufacturing a single pencil. He illustrates the miraculous, interconnected nature of a free market at work in the production of one seemingly insignificant item.

CHAPTER 11

Worthy of Praise

B eyond the inter-workings of capitalism, what are some of the broader effects of prosperity over the last century? Since 1800 the average life expectancy has nearly doubled and real income has increased nearly tenfold.

In 1900 almost no one had running water, central heating, electric washing machines, and refrigerators. Today, of those Americans officially designated as "poor", 99% have electricity, running water, flush toilets, and refrigerators. Rivers, lakes, and air are all getting cleaner.

Over the last 60 years (since 1955), the world population has more than doubled. A scarcity mentality would suggest that such growth would lead to great shortages of goods and services, but the opposite has happened. The average human earned three times more money on an inflation-adjusted basis and ate one-third more calories of food. The average human is now more literate and educated and less likely to die as result of war, famine, murder or childbirth.[12]

To acknowledge these things is not to say that all is well with the world, to be blind to the real dangers of consumerism, or to turn a blind eye to real economic injustices occurring. But it is to say we will not automatically fall prey to the prevailing attitude of discontent, envy, ingratitude, and bitterness. We will open our eyes to injustices and shortcomings and seek to address them intentionally in our own financial decisions as we've discussed. But we will also have eyes fully open to just how blessed we are. That is a source of freedom in a stifling environment of anger and discontent.

And lest any of us think our own circumstances are so poor as to warrant a gloomy pessimism, we would be wise to recall that the Apostle Paul wrote many of the most joy-filled passages in all of western literature while confined to abysmal conditions in a prison cell. In Philippians 4:8 he makes sure we understand where our focus should be:

> *"Finally, brothers, whatever is true, whatever is honorable, whatever is just, whatever is pure, whatever is lovely, whatever is commendable, if there is any excellence, if there is anything worthy of praise, think about these things."* – Philippians 4:8

It's not fashionable to defend capitalism or the free markets. It's also not fashionable to be awestruck or filled with wonder about anything and certainly not something as seemingly insignificant as a pencil. But I suggest we do it anyway because I think that is what Paul is telling us to do.

We, as followers of Jesus, should embrace the unfashionable and the counter-cultural. Let's not be afraid to be labeled "true believers" and take the scary step of actually believing in things and being filled with child-like wonder at the miraculousness of the ordinary.

Psychotherapist Amy Morin, who became a widow at the age of 26, says the key to mental strength is to *"affirm the good in the world, and you will begin to appreciate what you have,"* and goes on to say: *"The goal is to swap self-pity with gratitude."* [13]

Gratitude is the antidote because we can either be angry at not getting what we deserved or elated at not getting what we deserved. As sinners in need of a savior, our attitude should be much more reflective of the latter mindset.

CHAPTER 12

Radicalized By Gratitude

L eviticus 25:10 instructed God's people to "proclaim liberty throughout the land" by returning all land to the original owners every 50th year. This was referred to as the year of "Jubilee." In *The Upside-Down Kingdom*, Donald Kraybill makes a strong case that the concept of Jubilee infused Jesus' self-described identity and mission and cites Luke 4:18-19 as an example: [14]

> *"The Spirit of the Lord is upon me, because he has anointed me to bring good news to the poor. He has sent me to proclaim release to the captives and recovery of sight to the blind, to let the oppressed go free, to proclaim the year of the Lord's favor."*

Jubilee is meant to remind us that we are forgiven debtors. We were once oppressed. We were once captives. We were once slaves who are now freed. And our response, in turn, as followers of Jesus is to extend that grace and forgiveness to others.

The essence of this concept of Jubilee is central to the Lord's Prayer. Scholars note that the word "debts" may refer to either sins or financial debts. And Jesus' parable of the unforgiving servant emphasizes this need to remember debts forgiven.

In Matthew 18:23-25, when a king forgives a huge debt of his servant, that servant proceeds to turn around and physically threaten and abuse a fellow servant for not repaying a much smaller debt he is owed. It illustrates how easily we can forget the deep spiritual debt that was paid on our behalf.

Ultimately, the immense grace bestowed on us should propel us to show the same spirit of forgiveness and grace to others. This is evidenced when Jesus instructs us to ask our Heavenly Father to *"forgive us our debts as we forgive our debtors."* As Kraybill points out, *"The Jubilee Principle of reciprocal forgiveness pervades the New Testament teaching."*

The more we are animated by the abundance of God's grace and love for us, the more we will be motivated to extend generosity to others by following the pattern of God's people who throughout history forgave debts, freed slaves, and returned land. This grace-infused giving is not concerned with an ROI (return on investment). It is witnessed by giving money away with no strings attached and no expectations for what the money need be used for.

It is instructive to consider that Jesus had an entirely different economy than we do. He is not easily put into a box. The same son of God who did not have a place to lay his head and seemed relatively unconcerned about basic provisions beyond his daily needs was also one who encouraged feasts and celebration. His first miracle, after all, was to turn water into wine at a wedding that was already well underway. His frugality co-mingled with his extravagance.

Jesus showed us how to live in such a way that money is stripped of its power over us. In a culture obsessed with all of the trappings of wealth, he offers insight for how to smash the idol of money.

The beginning of Matthew 26 recounts the story of a woman who pours a very expensive bottle of ointment on the head of Jesus. When she did this, several of the disciples became indignant and asked why she would "waste" it like that and went on to lament how it could have been sold and the proceeds given to the poor instead. Jesus rebuked them and said she had done a good work for him and prepared him for his burial. How many of us would react similarly to the disciples? ("Think of all the things we could do with that money!")

At least part of the lesson here is that we should guard ourselves against the impulse to always have to maximize our returns on generosity. The giving in this story, much like that which Christ showed throughout the Gospel accounts, was grace-based. The woman understood how deep her debt to Jesus was and how extensive his grace had been and, as a result, she gave out of that same sense of grace – overflowing and uncalculating.

The minister and family wealth counselor Jay Link contrasts the ideal of "generous giving by faith" with a "legalistic giving by math." He says we should avoid the three pharisaical inclinations: giving with guilt, giving legalistically to the penny, and giving with pride.

I like the way Father Aquinas Guilbeau (from the Dominican House of Studies in Washington, D.C.) puts it when he says we are *"radicalized by gratitude."* He explains that gratitude uproots us *"from pride and self-centeredness."* It *"requires a recognition of the debt we owe to others, which, touching the most important things in life – like life itself – is a debt we cannot repay."*[15]

Freedom is evidenced when we voluntarily limit the amount of money we will spend on ourselves out of love for others and a life-shaping desire to be more generous. This is very different than asking how much scripture requires of us to give away in a law-based mentality about giving.

CHAPTER 13

Eternal Rewards

In one of his sermons, John Piper recalled watching news coverage of Vietnam prisoners of war reuniting with their spouses after years in captivity. He explained the emotional effect of seeing videos of wives and children running to embrace these soldiers whom they had long feared were dead.

Piper then asked that we turn the clock back two weeks earlier. Imagine the wife of one of these soldiers receiving a phone call informing her that her husband is alive and will be coming home in two weeks. She's been faithful for six years during which time her hopes had greatly dimmed. Six years went by and there was no information about her husband – whether he was alive or dead. Then the phone rings...

None of her circumstances actually changed with that phone call. Everything was exactly as it was before. But, yet, everything changed. The difference was simply the news she had received. There was now a real hope. Her husband was alive! The father of her children would be reunited with them. In two weeks, she would hold him. The news she received changed her entire reality. She did not need anyone to teach her to be joyful or reorient her life. [16]

We want to learn the right principles. We want steps to financial success. We want to understand what we have to do to enjoy more security and more freedom. But Jesus says we are asking for the wrong things. He says what we really need – what will really fulfill us – is not good advice but good news.

The Bible is not intended to merely inform us, but to transform us. It is centered on the Good News of God's new world breaking into this one and undoing death and injustice. Jesus is setting the world right and the sad things are coming untrue. It is not enough to know the gospel in our heads; we need it to penetrate our hearts.

In Colossians 3:4, we learn *"When Christ, our life, is revealed, then you will also be revealed with him in glory."* Scripture is promising that one day we will become who we were meant to be: radiant, glorious image-bearers of God. God invites us into this unmerited future as an act of pure grace. If we set this hope before us, it will radically reshape our lives and give us eyes to see the eternal significance of our daily actions.

In *A Christmas Carol*, Charles Dickens portrayed the transformation of Ebeneezer Scrooge from a heartless indifference toward the suffering of others to an overflowing generosity which led to cherishing every single encounter with anyone in his path. Not unlike George Bailey in *It's a Wonderful Life*, Scrooge was profoundly changed by gaining an eternal perspective. It revealed, as C.S. Lewis put it, *"There are no ordinary people. You have never talked to a mere mortal."* [17]

The implication is that every moment truly matters and pursuit of earthly riches is seen for what it is: trivial and fleeting. May we, too, be graced with a proper reordering of our loves which redeems our relationship with money.

ACKNOWLEDGMENTS

O ne of the most important things for me in the process of writing is to know that I am not alone; that there are other like-minded travelers on a similar journey. This was especially true given certain subject matter in this book.

Over the course of the last two decades, I've been indoctrinated with a certain way of thinking about wealth management. It was very difficult to fundamentally challenge the prevailing mindset of an industry and, in fact, the only way for me to persevere was to listen and collaborate with others who are not content to accept conventional wisdom.

To talk with those who yearn for a more redemptive conception of topics that affect our lives on a daily basis. To be part of a dialogue that asks how we faithfully follow Jesus in two of the most important aspects of our lives: work and money. To collaborate with those who desperately desire to imagine what could be rather than begrudgingly accept what is.

I first want to thank my wife, Jennifer, for her love and support, and for helping me to communicate in plain English so that people can understand what I'm trying to say.

I am thankful for so many who have offered helpful feedback from my first book, which helped shape what topics I would address here and how I would do so. I won't be able to name everyone, but the list includes my dad and my sister as well as the following people: Jerry Webb, Jeremy Briell, Angela Granata, Nicole Stephan, Ben & Heidi Kinsella, Ed Briscoe, and Mike Dineen.

Over the course of the last year, I have been blessed to get to know Jeff Haanen and the amazing things that he is doing at Denver Institute for Faith & Work, the organization he founded several years ago. I believe that Jeff, along with Joanna Meyer and others at Denver Institute, will continue to be a blessing for those who want to have a truly biblical perspective on why work matters to God and put into action many of the ideas I have tried to articulate here.

Speaking of putting ideas into action, I'd like to thank the many people in the faith-based investing community who have been great resources. In particular, I have learned a lot from John Siverling, Executive Director of the Christian Investment Forum as well as Robin John, Tim Weinhold, and Jeff Cave at Eventide Funds.

Finally, I'm thankful for the leadership and community of believers at Denver Presbyterian Church. It has been a huge influence on my own beliefs and how I seek to integrate faith with all aspects of life.

NOTES

INTRODUCTION

1 "Pathologies of the Idle Rich, Part 3," *Slate*. Virginia: Graham Holdings Company, March 12, 2001.

2 Aldrich, Nelson. *Old Money*. New York: Allworth Press, 1997.

3 Sedgwick, John. *Rich Kids: America's Young Heirs & Heiresses, How They Love & Hate Their Money*. New York: William Morrow & Company, 1985.

4 Dylan, Bob. "Like a Rolling Stone," *Highway 61 Revisited*. New York: Columbia Records, 1965.

5 Joplin, Janis. "Me and My Bobby McGee," *Pearl*. New York: Columbia Records, 1971.

6 Wallace, David Foster. (2005, May). "This is Water," Speech presented at Kenyon College, Gambier, OH.

7 Szalavitz, Maia. "What Does a 400% Increase in Antidepressant Use Really Mean?" *Time Magazine*. 10/20/2011.

8 Wallace, David Foster. (2005, May). "This is Water," Speech presented at Kenyon College, Gambier, OH.

9 Turner, Frank. "The Road," *Poetry of the Dead*. London: Xtra Mile Recordings, 2009.

10 Belsky, Scott. *Making Ideas Happen*. London: Portfolio; Reprint edition, 2012.

11 Gelinas, Robert. *Finding the Groove*. Michigan: Zondervan, 2009.

SECTION I

1 Wilde, Oscar. *The Picture of Dorian Gray*. New York: Dover Publications; Reprint edition, 1993.

2 Chesterton, G.K. *Tremendous Trifles*. New York: Dover Publications; Reprint edition, 2007.

3 Gallup Daily Tracking: U.S. Engagement, 5/3/16.

4 Terkel, Studs. *Working*. New York: The New Press, 1997.

5 Sayers, Dorothy. "Why Work," *Letters to a Diminished Church: Passionate Arguments for the Relevance of Christian Doctrine*. 1942. Nashville, TN: Thomas Nelson, 2004.

6 Crawford, Matthew. *Shop Class as Soulcraft*. London: Penguin Books; Reprint edition, 2010.

7 Terkel, Studs. *Working.* New York: The New Press, 1997.

8 Brooks, Katharine. "Job, Career, Calling: Key to Happiness and Meaning at Work?" *Psychology Today.* 6/29/2012.

9 Schwartz, Barry. "The Way We Think About Work is Broken." TED. Sept. 2015. Lecture.

10 Barnett, Bill. "Make Your Job More Meaningful," *Harvard Business Review.* 4/12/2012.

11 Sturt, David. *Great Work.* New York: McGraw-Hill Education, 2013.

12 Haanen, Jeff. "Moving West for Meaningful Work," *Daily Camera.* 1/26/2016.

13 McCampbell, Mary. "Policing with Embrace: How Officer Norman Loves His Community," *Christ & Pop Culture.* 8/18/2015.

14 "Transformation Textiles: Secure & Comfortable FHP Solutions for Global Impact," Skillshare.com, 1/15/2014.

15 Thomashauer, Regena. "Giving Back to Our Sisters Worldwide," MamaGenas.com, 12/23/2014.

16 "Faith Meets the Entrepreneurial Spirit," *Christianity Today.* 8/10/2015.

17 Isaacson, Walter. Steve Jobs. New York: Simon & Schuster, 2015.

18 Augustine, St. *The Confessions of Saint Augustine.* New York: Image Classics, 1960.

19 Schulevitz, Judith. "Bring Back the Sabbath," *New York Times.* 3/2/2003.

SECTION II

1 Chu, Jeff. "Kenneth Cole on Why Going Private Was the Smartest Thing He Ever Did," *Inc. Magazine.* November 2015.

2 Duzer, Jeff Van. *Why Business Matters to God.* Illinois: IVP Academic, 2010.

3 Collins, Jim & Porra, Jerry. *Built to Last: Successful Habits of Visionary Companies.* New York: HarperCollins Publishers, 1994.

4 Sisodia, Raj &Wolfe, David B. & Sheth, Jag. *Firms of Endearment: How World-Class Companies Profit from Passion & Purpose.* New Jersey: Wharton School Publishing, 2007.

5 Reichheld, Frank. *The Ultimate Question: Driving Good Profits & True Growth.* Massachusetts: Harvard Business Review Press, 2006.

6 "SRI Basics," *The Forum for Sustainable and Responsible Investment.* USSIF.org.

7 "Important Element: Giving Back," *U.S. Trust Insights on Wealth and Worth.* Bank of America Corporation, 2015.

8 Pearcey, Nancy. *Total Truth*. Illinois: Crossway, 2008.

9 Ramsey, Dave. "Dave's Investing Philosophy," *DaveRamsey.com*. 6/14/2009.

10 "Great Expectations: Mission Preservation and Financial Performance in Impact Investments," Wharton School of the University of Pennsylvania. 10/7/2015.

11 Openshaw, Jennifer. "'Socially Responsible' Investing Has Beaten the S&P 500 for Decades," MarketWatch.com, 5/26/2015.

12 *Shedding Light on Responsible Investment: Approaches, Returns, and Impacts*. London: Mercer Research, 2009.

13 "The Business Case for Sustainable Investing," Morgan Stanley, 4/28/2015.

14 Dalbar *Quantitative Analysis of Investor Behavior (20th Ed.)*. Boston, 2014.

15 Hamilton, Chad. "Make Sure Emotions Don't Override Logic in Financial Decisions," *Marketwatch.com*. 4/29/16.

16 "Important Element: Giving Back," *U.S. Trust Insights on Wealth and Worth*. Bank of America Corporation, 2015.

17 Siverling, John. "Bridging a Great Divide: The Evolving Evangelical Relationship with SRI," *GreenMoney Journal*. February 2015.

18 "Is there really a market for BRI funds?" *ChristianInvestment-Forum.com.* Frequently Asked Questions.

19 Weinhold, Tim. "Investing That Prospers," EvenTideFunds.com, 9/29/14.

20 Taylor, Bill. "The Best Entrepreneurs Are Missionaries, Not Mercenaries," *Harvard Business Review.* 4/11/2016.

21 Lupkin, Sydney. "How a Family Car Wash Has Changed the Lives of People with Autism," *ABCNews.com.* 2/10/2015.

22 Spence, Roy M., Jr. *It's Not What You Sell, It's What You Stand For.* New York: Penguin Group, 2009.

23 "Southwest Airlines 'Gets It' With Our Culture," BlogSouth-West.com, 3/22/2011.

24 "Helping Potted Plants Grow," Everence.com. Investments: February 2016.

25 Regier, Mark. "More than Materiality: The SRI-ESG Conversation," *GreenMoney Journal.* February 2015.

SECTION III

1 Brooks, David. *The Road to Character.* New York: Random House, 2015.

2 Jayson, Sharon. "Generation Y's Goal? Wealth and Fame," *USA Today.* 1/10/2007.

3 Becker, Ernest. *The Denial of Death.* New York: Free Press, 1997.

4 Brooks, David. *The Road to Character.* New York: Random House, 2015.

5 Noonan, Peggy. "A Life's Lesson," *The Wall Street Journal.* 6/20/2008.

6 Ferguson, Sinclair. *Grow in Grace.* Edinburg, Scotland: Banner of Truth Publishing, 1989.

7 Foster, Richard. *The Challenge of the Disciplined Life.* New York: HarperOne, 1989.

8 Ellul, Jacques. Money & Power. Oregon: Wipf & Stock Publishing, 2009.

9 Brown, Brenee. *Daring Greatly.* New York: Avery, 2015.

10 Stephens, Bret. "Hillary's Cynical Song of Self," *The Wall Street Journal.* 4/27/2015.

11 Read, Leonard E. "I, Pencil: My Family Tree as Told to Leonard E. Read," *The Freeman.* 1958.

12 Ridley, Matt. *The Rational Optimist: How Prosperity Evolves.* New York: Harper Perennial; Reprint edition, 2011.

13 Morin, Amy. *13 Things Mentally Strong People Don't Do*. New York: William Morrow Publishing, 2014.

14 Kraybill, Donald. *The Upside-Down Kingdom*. Maryland: Herald Press; 5th Updated edition, 2011.

15 Lopez, Kathryn Jean. *National Review*. 2/29/2016.

16 Piper, John. "Let Us Exult in the Hope of the Glory of God!" (Romans 5:1-2) *Romans: The Greatest Letter Ever Written*. 10/24/99.

17 Lewis, C. S. *The Weight of Glory*. New York: HarperOne; 2/13/01 edition.

32554478R00091

Made in the USA
Middletown, DE
08 June 2016